Deadly Down Under

Derek Underwood

Deadly Down Under

Photographs by Eric Piper

Arthur Barker Limited London
A subsidiary of Weidenfeld (Publishers) Limited

I would like to thank Chris Lander, without whom this book would not have been possible. His humour, wit and elusiveness contributed in no small way to a lot of fun on the tour and I wish him every success in the future.

Derek Underwood, May 1980

Published in Great Britain by Arthur Barker Limited
91 Clapham High Street, London SW4 7TA

ISBN 0 213 16777 8

Printed in Great Britain at
The Camelot Press Ltd, Southampton

Contents

To my wife Dawn,
my children Heather and Fiona,
and all those who have been so understanding
throughout the last two years.

1. To Australia with England

My life as a professional cricketer turned full circle when Phil Edmonds came and told me I had been chosen for the England Tour of Australia. Having been a fairly prominent member of the England team throughout the seventies, I had gone into voluntary Test exile as a World Series cricketer for two and a half years and, happily, was selected to play for my country again.

The experience of those thirty months was unbelievable and I can honestly say that despite the drama on and off the field I have no regrets about having signed for World Series Cricket in April 1977. Not regretting such a momentous decision should not mislead the cricketing public into imagining that I didn't have misgivings about my involvement in a series of events that turned the world of professional cricket upside down.

The advent of WSC could be traced in the growing pockets of discontent to be found in most dressing-rooms occupied by international cricket teams, and county sides too. Kerry Packer lured the world's fifty or so best cricketers by appealing to them in many directions, and in one area that was sensitive to them all.

His package was hard to resist for even the better paid Test player; most players worked out they would earn around £10,000 for three months' work plus perks and, in most cases, the promise of at least a two-year and probably a three-year contract.

Attractive as this deal was, money was not the only motivating factor that led to my decision to join WSC. There were several aspects that appealed to my wife, Dawn, and myself, including the promise of security for my family for three successive winters.

Even though I had played seventy times for England at that stage I was well aware of the insecurities of professional cricket. Although I had been in the England side for the best part of ten years it was not until 1976 against the West Indies at home that I played in a full series.

The Ashes-winning tour of Australia in 1970–71, under Ray Illingworth, provided a classic example of the way one's Test future could be so uncertain just when it seemed one was settled as a permanent member of the team.

My contribution in that series had been seventeen wickets. We went to New Zealand where I took twelve wickets in the Christchurch Test and five in New Zealand's first innings at Auckland. Back in England the next summer, in the first Test against Pakistan at Edgbaston, I bowled 41 overs finishing with 0–102. I thought that I had done as well as anyone in the face of Zaheer Abbas during his incredible innings of 274, yet I found myself dropped for the next Test, and there have been numerous other instances similar to this in my career.

Now I was being guaranteed three winters of cricket in Australia, a country I enjoyed being in and where I liked playing the game. At thirty-two, it was important to be realistic and admit to being in the twilight of my career, for there were not likely to be many offers to rival this one.

For the first time in fifteen years as a professional cricketer I knew where I stood, knew what I was doing, and it was possible to plan ahead. After all, there were no promises of remaining a Test player nor were there any loyalty clauses for making oneself available for the winter. Now there was a rewarding future on several fronts.

WSC were generous in helping our families join us in Australia, particularly important to me at the time because Dawn was expecting our second daughter, Fiona.

From a strict cricketing point of view it was an enormous honour being chosen for the World XI against Australia who were, arguably, the strongest side in the world when we took them on in the Centenary Test in Melbourne in March 1977. The excitement of being part of such a revolutionary development in international cricket was also an attractive incentive.

WSC's original plan was for Australia to take on the world in a series of six 'Super-Tests' involving a squad of seventeen players.

Later decisions to recruit the whole West Indies team and to concentrate on money-making, one-day matches made it increasingly hard for me to command a place in the World XI during the second season. We had a whole range of express fast bowlers – John Snow, Mike Procter, Imran Khan, Sarfraz Nawaz, Garth Le Roux and Clive Rice backed up by Asif Iqbal and Tony Greig, captain of the World XI – so that I became almost redundant in one-day games. Often I finished up as twelfth man, the spinner being omitted, a trait which has sadly permeated Test cricket in most parts of the world, with India still notably the exception.

After all the novelty of these games and some highly competitive cricket played in deadly earnest for large sums of prize-money, the World XI, with its assorted combination of nationalities, had no real identity for the public. Who would support the world?

We could not muster the kind of team spirit associated with bona fide Test cricket, although the games were played in a highly competitive manner, and this aspect made me miss playing for England as much as anything and sometimes made me think how much I would love to have been back in the England side chasing Lance Gibb's world record of 309 Test wickets.

The World XI also feared that the introduction of the West Indies side would undermine their position and force them to play less glamorous matches out in country areas, while Australia and the West Indies competed in front of bigger crowds in the major cities.

The greatest pressures on the English WSC players – Tony Greig, John Snow, Dennis Amiss, Alan Knott, Bob Woolmer and myself – were felt at home. The Australians and the West Indians were in a very different position, having signed more or less *en bloc* whereas we took the full brunt and fury of the cricketing establishment as an isolated group and found the Players Union, the Professional Cricketers' Association, in virtually unanimous opposition to us.

During England's tour of Pakistan and New Zealand, in the winter of 1977–8, the England players drew up a list of proposals aimed mainly at WSC men. Happily these motions were shelved early in the summer of 1978 when Kerry Packer's visiting emissaries talked about a settlement between cricket's opposing factions.

The first time I heard of anything connected with Kerry Packer's ideas for WSC came in a surprise telephone call from Tony Greig the morning after he was the subject of the 'This is Your Life' television programme. At the end of the show he asked me if he could ring me first thing in the morning as he had something important to discuss with me.

I shall always remember sleeping uneasily that night wondering what on earth Tony was talking about. At about eight o'clock the next morning he called me back and broadly outlined Packer's ideas. It sounded very exciting.

A few days later, Tony was in touch again asking me to attend a meeting at the Churchill Hotel in London where a small group of players and key officials got together. Most of the talking was done by Austin Robertson, one of the founder members, the others being John Cornell and Paul Hogan, both well-known Australian television comedians. They represented JP Sports Limited, with whom our original contracts were drawn up.

Cornell's business connections with Dennis Lillee really triggered off the idea of WSC. He was amazed how badly top cricketers were being paid.

The English players at that historic gathering were Tony Greig, John Snow, Alan Knott and myself, with South Africans Mike Procter, Barry Richards, Graeme Pollock and Denys Hobson also in attendance.

One of the biggest topics debated was the implication of joining such a breakaway group and we talked about how we would be risking our Test careers. The English players had the most to lose because we would not be available for any tours abroad during the next two or three winters.

I remember saying to Greig, 'Over your dead body – this is quite something that we're going into. I just hope it all works.' But he was as full of enthusiasm and confidence as ever about this radical scheme which, though we did not realize it, was going to disrupt conventional cricket all round the world.

Later that night, after we'd barely digested the proposals, we all took off for the Dorchester Hotel where we were to meet Kerry Packer for the first time. Packer reassured us in the most convincing manner that we would be looked after in return for our cricketing services during three seasons in Australia and I signed my contract there and then.

My next move was to confirm that my contract with Kent, my principal employers, did not in any way bar me from joining WSC. Ironically, because of the selective employment tax system of a few years ago, English professional cricketers were mostly engaged on contracts that ran from April until September which meant they were not tied to their counties during the winter months. How different it might have been had we been retained on an annual basis!

I was anxious to ensure that I was not breaking any of the stringent rules and regulations laid down by the Test and

County Cricket Board, but my solicitors could find nothing that would stop me from going off to Australia that winter. It was comforting to know that legally there was nothing to stop us playing in this unique series of cricket matches.

A fortnight later the news broke during a match between Sussex and the Australians at Hove, after Tony Greig had thrown a party at his home and the gossip among Australian players and journalists had become more than just well-founded rumours. Ian Wooldridge wrote cricket's most dramatic story of the century in the *Daily Mail* on Monday, 9 May and all hell broke loose.

I realized my Test career would be in jeopardy once I had signed and it may well be because of my cautious nature that I was the lone voice among Greig, Knott, Snow and Amiss in predicting that the counties would react against us. None of us were in any doubt about the risks we were taking in terms of remaining England players. What was to hurt me most was the reaction within Kent County Cricket Club, which had been so much my life since the early 1960s. Initially they raised no objections to my going off to Australia. I had informed our Chairman, Walter Brice, the day WSC was announced publicly and his reaction was 'Fair enough', provided it did not conflict with my agreement with Kent.

Mr Brice came to Lord's during the game against Middlesex and discussed the whole matter of WSC with Knotty, Asif Iqbal and myself. No county was affected in quite the same way as Kent were. The overall reaction to our joining WSC was a mixture of bewilderment and resentment in those early days when very few people realized the sort of impact that it would have and how it was to divide cricketers and lovers of the game all over the world.

The people who signed for WSC thought that the world's cricket authorities were rather naïve in accusing us of going about it in such a 'furtive way', but did they really imagine the enterprise could be set up if it had been announced to the whole world?

As that fateful summer of 1977 went on, Packer's recruiting of the cream of the world's Test cricketers hardened the feeling against us. It became obvious that conventional Test cricket faced an enormous threat.

Tony Greig, to nobody's surprise, had now been sacked as England captain but we all remained England players, of course aware that our involvement would be at an end when that series was over against Australia. Greig was under more pressure than any of us because he was our spokesman and the principal link between WSC and English cricket and, having acted the way he did while still England captain, was regarded as the game's greatest traitor.

When we look back now at the biggest revolution professional cricket has ever undergone, we hope that those who were so violently against WSC appreciate how we helped improve the lot of professional cricketers everywhere. Nobody can claim that it is pure coincidence the way England's and Australia's best players are now so much better paid. In England, we have substantial sponsorship of Test cricket from Cornhill, the insurance group; Test fees have increased to £1,400 and loyalty contracts now afford England players more money and greater security. Moreover, increasing amounts of sponsorhip money have benefited the average county cricketer who is at last guaranteed a living minimum wage.

The hardening reaction of the principal international cricketing bodies against WSC and their attitude of 'Packer's not going to beat us; we'll fight him, we'll destroy him' developed into an unfortunate and costly High Court case.

I for one was desperately sad that it had to come to a situation where professional cricketers were brought into court and had to defend their rights to play a new version of professional cricket. Asif Iqbal and I made a point of making sure that one of us was in court every day to monitor everything that happened during the thirty-one days of the hearing.

The establishment must have regretted letting the case go to court because it cost them over £250,000 after they lost on every count. When we reflected on the original argument about Kerry Packer wanting to acquire exclusive television rights for showing cricket in Australia, it seemed incredible that the cricketing bodies could not have resolved the problems without going to court. The irony was the way English cricket bore the brunt of what was essentially an Australian problem!

Nothing hurt me personally as much as the intensity of feeling over the whole affair in my own county of Kent.

There was such a wide division of opinion among County members and feelings ran so deeply and emotionally that many personal relationships were affected. The most shattering episode for Asif, Knott, Woolmer and myself was when the four of us were informed we were not to be offered contracts at the end of the 1978 season. The timing of this decision was all the more staggering as it came before we had even started that summer's cricket. John Pocock, Chairman of the Cricket Committee, took Bob Woolmer and myself aside at Canterbury and told us that we would not be required for 1979. We just could not believe that all we had done for Kent in the years before could be discounted in a two and a half hour meeting. To say their action was hurtful was the understatement of the year. What we could not fathom was why we should be dismissed from Kent simply because we wanted to play cricket under another banner in another part of the world during the winter.

They talked about our disloyalty to Kent and we wondered just where their loyalties lay. I reckoned, without being conceited, that I had contributed to Kent's post-war success as much as any other bowler and yet here I was being fired from a club I had served in what I thought was a dedicated way for sixteen seasons.

Kent Committee's attitude was that they did not want to retain us because of our involvement with WSC which they saw as a threat to Test cricket. To an extent, we understood their concern because the people who were against us also feared for the future of county cricket. The counties virtually depend on the money distributed in large amounts from Test match attendance and television rights. Because Test cricket was being disrupted they felt threatened and thought they could get at WSC through us.

It made it all the more perverse that Kent should win the Schweppes County Championship and Benson and Hedges Cup that summer with four key players who knew they were to be sacked. I found I was living on a knife-edge, especially in terms of the hostility and pressures off the field. I tried not to take it personally, but it worried me more than most as to how people reacted to our joining WSC. Some were so angry that they didn't want to be confronted with me in conversation and in some respects this awkward atmosphere still exists.

Luckily I was able to divorce myself from the never-ending arguments by shutting them out of my mind when we were actually out there playing for Kent. It helped that I received a great deal of sympathy and understanding from my Kent team-mates, otherwise I'm sure I could never have taken over 200 wickets in the next two seasons. Even though we had won the Championship in 1978, our success was not greeted as well in some quarters – an admission even made in the President's Report – as it would have been if Kent had not relied on their WSC men.

I found that attitude small-minded and upsetting. I look upon those wickets in 1978 and 1979 as being my crowning achievement for Kent, yet they were appreciated with muffled gratitude. I remember thinking that should I never play for Kent again after 1978 the best way would be to go out in a blaze of glory by taking 100 wickets.

The last thing I wanted was for people to feel I'd turned my back completely on Kent. Gradually during these fraught months, there was a swelling in the ranks of those who did realize we had been loyal to the County down the years.

Les Ames, Kent's former Secretary/Manager, and an outstanding Kent and England cricketer in the pre-war era, was one man who fought bravely for our being retained by the County. He had an awful lot to lose but had the courage to stand up at the Annual Meeting and say publicly that he was appalled by our dismissal. He was not alone in his views, having the support of many ex-cricketers on the committee.

What he said and did led to a more sympathetic approach towards the WSC players and probably influenced the reversal of the committee's earlier decision. I got the impression that many people had a change of heart, fearing that we might bring a lawsuit against the County for wrongful dismissal and if we did want such an action it would have been the members of the committtee who would have been liable for costs! There were suggestions that Kent's WSC players had threatened to boycott the Benson and Hedges final against Derbyshire if we were not re-engaged for 1979. That was nonsense; it was pure coincidence that Kent offered us new terms around that time.

One factor that influenced our retention by Kent was that other counties like Gloucestershire (Mike Procter and Zaheer), Hampshire (Gordon Greenidge, Barry Richards and Andy Roberts), Lancashire (Clive Lloyd), Middlesex (Wayne Daniel), Notts (Clive Rice) and Somerset (Viv Richards) wanted to keep their WSC players. Kent, who had a tradition of success and wanted to guard it jealously, could not bear the thought of my joining another county and playing against them.

Kent cricket has been the basis of my life and in spite of the trauma and unhappiness over the last couple of years, I hope it will continue to be. With the tension relaxing a little between WSC and cricket's official authorities, we were able to regard the possibility of returning to Test cricket when the 1979 season opened. It occurred to me that taking 100 wickets for Kent would be a mighty strong argument for my recall after the tour of Australia, so I set my sights on this target.

With the help of one bad batting performance and a good wicket to bowl on near the end of the season, I just made it. Even then, the situation was still in the balance with the selectors being urged not to reinstate the 'Packer defectors', as we were still referred to in some quarters.

The Underwood family will never forget Sunday, 9 September 1979, nor I suppose will Phil Edmonds. It would be hard to recall a more emotional or more embarrassing off-the-field cricket situation with another player.

It came as momentous news to both of us and must have been heartbreaking for Phil, who had been a regular member of the England side since my joining WSC.

I cherished the news even more because I had prepared myself to expect the worst, knowing the extreme depths of anti-Packer feeling up and down the country. With the England captain, Mike Brearley, and Phil in the Middlesex side playing us at Canterbury that day, I sensed I might hear something about the tour party for Australia.

Officially the names of the sixteen lucky players were being announced the next day so I thought I'd have to wait until Monday morning either to hear the team announced on the radio or to get a letter through the post.

We had just lost a game that was to cost us the John Player League title and I was looking for a vacant shower when Phil walked by and said, 'Congratulations, Derek, you're going to Australia.'

I had to admire him for coming and telling me, and thought it said a lot for his strength of character. We both knew each other's feelings and my rather stuttering reply was, 'Thanks, Phil, I don't know what to say.'

There I was standing in the shower letting the marvellous news sink in when Paul Downton, our wicketkeeper, relayed a message that the England captain wanted a word with me.

Mike Brearley then gave me the official nod with his best wishes and I was to discover later that the critical meeting of selectors – Alec Bedser, Ken Barrington, Charlie Elliott, Brian Close, plus the Captain – had lasted for over seven hours. It came as no surprise that my inclusion linked with Edmond's omission had occupied a large part of that selection debate.

In the last two months of the season I had learned to live with all the furore about my possible return to the England team. It had become a burning issue with past and present England cricketers and I was used to headlines like: 'Dare They Take Derek?' and 'Should Deadly Really Come Back?'

For Phil Edmonds it was really tough. He has improved vastly over the past couple of years and has two great strengths over me in his batting, which has developed so much, and in his close-to-the-wicket fielding. They are factors which will keep Phil very much in the running and we could well play for England in the same side in the future just as we did against Australia at Leeds in 1975 when Phil was the new boy.

After hearing that the cricket establishment had finally pardoned me and, concealing my delight for team-mate Graham Dilley's selection, I withdrew to think, standing aside in a corner of the pavilion at our end of the season drinks party. It was a moment to absorb everything that had happened since Kerry Packer first stunned the orderly world of cricket. Here I was, the only WSC man to be recalled by England after fearing and believing that the wheel would never turn full circle for me.

WSC players like Amiss, Alan Knott and Bob Woolmer were doubly aware that there would be no automatic recall and we knew we would have to earn our places.

Whatever the appeal of WSC's commercialism, the slick

presentation of their brand of cricket, the high stakes and privilege of playing alongside so many great players, the prime honour must still be playing for one's country. There can be no greater excitement than leading the England side off the field, having contributed towards a victory. My most treasured moment is the final Test at the Oval in 1968 when I took 7 for 50 against Australia.

Alec Bedser, Mike Brearley and their co-selectors had paid me the ultimate tribute as a person and cricketer. The anxiety to get out to Australia and, hopefully, justify their confidence and faith, was really building up.

2. The Build-Up to the Tour

A doctor's surgery around the corner from Lord's of all places was the scene of the most scary incident between the announcement of the tour party and the day we flew from London.

The tension in my mind about coming back to play for England was confirmed in the most unnerving way the day I went for my medical. I followed Geoff Miller in to see the doctor and could hardly believe what I was to be told a few minutes later. We were being checked by a woman doctor who told me my blood pressure was far too high for her to pass me fit for the tour. I thought, my God, I'm going to miss the tour.

She advised me to take a quiet walk for half an hour but I stayed in the surgery where she made me feel at ease after I'd joked, 'Maybe my blood pressure's up because I'm not used to being seen by a woman doctor!' She asked me whether I'd been worried at home and whether I had problems on my mind apart from my duties as a professional cricketer. This helped because I was able to explain my unusual situation as the only WSC player who'd been recalled to play for England. When she took my pressure again it had gone down sufficiently for her to pass me fit.

My nerves hadn't been good at all towards the end of the season and I still felt strangely unsettled, even after the tour party had been made known.

We were moving house too, and I'd had trouble selling my home. I have to admit at times the children got on top of me; I couldn't relax, I was over-emotional and even tearful. I couldn't sleep properly and actually finished up on Valium before we left for Australia, something I'd never resorted to in all my time in cricket.

All sorts of things were running through my mind and I realized that the pressure of putting so much into getting back into the team had taken more out of me than I realized. The telephone never stopped ringing with people saying 'Well done', and although I appreciated their good wishes it got to the stage where it almost proved too much for me. It revived memories of the first time I ever played for England back in 1966 when I think I counted 180 congratulatory telegrams and over 150 letters. It made me feel as though I was starting out as a Test cricketer all over again.

I thought deeply about the implications of being the only WSC man to be officially pardoned by the England selectors. I wondered about the selectors' real feelings and views about my recall. Alan Knott, Bob Woolmer and myself were obviously a bit sceptical about our chances of returning to Test cricket when none of us got the call for the Prudential World Cup matches earlier in the summer, even though a truce had been reached between the established bodies and WSC.

We thought England might want to reinforce their team at that stage for the World Cup. After all, the West Indies had included all their WSC contingent. We had the impression that the TCCB had not been fully informed of the terms of the compromise and we also remembered the way they had stood by us in 1977 in the series against Australia after it was known we were going to play under the WSC banner that winter.

I thought of the alternatives confronting the selectors and weighed these along with the intensity of feeling that was still so great about the WSC situation. Maybe the selectors were being very shrewd in not pitching any of us back into the Test arena back home. It would have been far more difficult to come back, say, in the final Test at the Oval under the critical gaze of everyone and possibly being judged on what I did in one Test.

I presumed that they thought the best way to ease any of us back into the England side was on the tour where the process would be more gradual. Also, in fairness to Alec Bedser and Kenny Barrington, they knew I was a worrier and that I can be a bit sensitive. In a way, I suppose I dreaded being brought back during the summer, imagining the criticism of the media and fearing the attitude of the cricketing public. After being out for two years there would have been unbelievable pressure on me. Everything I did would have been scrutinized. My 100 wickets for Kent and everything I'd put into this season could then have been wasted.

People in Kent, including senior committee men, kept saying to me, 'Don't worry, they can't leave you out of the tour, you're still the best slow left-arm bowler in England, they must take you to Australia.'

I hadn't had a conversation with anyone in authority in cricket and felt very alone. I particularly wanted someone to tell me what the official line of thinking was about England's WSC players. I realized I'd made my bed and had to lie on it but still would have loved to have known the views of cricket's leading administrators. For instance, we'd heard that some of the selectors took the attitude 'It'll be over our dead bodies if WSC players are recalled.' The uncertainty of what would happen in the selection made me all the more determined to keep taking wickets so that they couldn't ignore me.

I often thought back to the toughest Australian tour of all, in 1974–5, and the nightmares England's batsmen suffered against Dennis Lillee and Jeff Thomson. Would the tour be like that again?

There was another intriguing aspect to the debate about one or more WSC men being reinstated for the tour: part of the deal struck between Kerry Packer and the ICC was that there should be no victimization of those who had signed for WSC. Would there have been repercussions if no WSC cricketer had been chosen to go to Australia?

My selection must have helped clear the air with the Australians. I was told in Australia that the Australians could have kicked up such a fuss and might have gone as far as refusing to play England, the alternative being a six-Test series against the West Indies with perhaps a third country brought in to the World Series Cup one-day international games.

Tony Greig revealed that the selectors had come desperately close to recalling a second WSC man, my Kent team-mate Alan Knott. Apparently Greig had been in touch with the Kent and England wicket-keeper in the course of their very close relationship. Alan explained how the selectors had a number of telephone conversations to him at his Herne Bay home during their marathon seven-hour meeting. Alan was prepared to go to Australia, but on being approached at such short notice felt his family should be allowed to accompany him. After lengthy debates and more telephone calls it appears the selectors changed their minds. Australian players later expressed their surprise that both Alan Knott and Bob Woolmer had been left behind.

On top of all this, the health of my mother during that summer had been a constant worry. She had attended the first match of the season – Champion County (Kent) v. MCC at Lord's – in the hope of seeing me take my first wicket of the summer. She had severe pains down her legs during this game and later had to have a major operation on her back. I remember dashing straight from the ground at Chelmsford after we had reduced the Championship Table leaders, Essex, to 9 for 43. We'd bowled on a wicket where I should have returned devastating figures. Instead, I took only 2 for 13 with off-spinner Graham Johnson doing a demolition job at the other end. Obviously my anxiety to get to the hospital to see my mother had affected my cricket. Happily, she has made a remarkable recovery.

Maybe because I took the overall criticism about our involvement with WSC so personally, I had been more upset by comments in all sections of the media, who seemed set on none of us being allowed to play for England again. I'd found it very difficult to communicate with most of the cricketing journalists and wondered whether they really meant it when they came up to me saying such things as, 'Nice to see you're on the tour, it's good that you are back again.' I thought, do they really mean it when for the past two years they've knocked me and said I shouldn't be picked for England again?

It didn't help when I had a confrontation with an ITN News crew who came to my new house in Sevenoaks. They seemed intent on causing friction and played on the relationship between the TCCB and WSC, asking me such questions as, 'If it wasn't for Packer, I don't suppose you would have been able to afford this nice house.' I asked if we could stick to talking about cricket but they only wanted to create a sensational item for that evening's programme news. They paid me £30 – I would willingly have given them the money back to get rid of them. Then they wanted pictures of my wife and children before the programme which, naturally, I wouldn't allow. To be honest, I later refused to give interviews to the same television interviewer on the tour.

One of the things that helped take worries off my mind was assisting my Kent colleague, Graham Dilley, very much the new boy on tour. He leaned on me and I was delighted to be able to advise him and have never forgotten his look of amazement when I told him, walking to the car-park at Canterbury that Sunday that we were both going to Australia. Mike Brearley had asked me to pass on the good news to Graham, making sure it remained confidential that night because the tour party was not being officially announced until the Monday morning.

In the days that lead up to going away on an England tour there is a mixture of excitement and dread. No one really relishes being separated from his family for four months, but at the same time there is the anticipation of the excitement of playing for one's country, the honour, the glory and the fun on tour. These feelings were much more intense on this occasion because of my anxiety about how I would be received by several England players who not so many months earlier had been doing their damnedest to pass motions that barred WSC cricketers from even playing in domestic cricket. After all, virtually the last time I had seen someone like Geoff Boycott was when he was in the High Court giving evidence on behalf of the TCCB in the case that will never be forgotten as long as cricket is played.

When we assembled at the indoor cricket school at Lord's to sort out all our clothing, gear and presents from various sponsors, I was still frightened and worried about pertinent questions being put by the media who had turned up en masse.

On the drive up to Lord's with Graham Dilley and his father, I'd reflected on happier moments and remembered that two of England's staunchest anti-WSC men, Bob Willis and John Lever, had taken the trouble to write to me from Pakistan two winters before when I was playing for WSC in Australia. They had sent me a very amusing letter from the Sainjees Hotel in Hyderabad saying it was the worst hotel in the world with no running water and beds with no springs in them! They added how 'comfortably' they were living and asked me if I remembered previous visits there. During the summer of 1977 I'd said to Bob and John, give the Sainjees my regards. Hyderabad was not exactly my favourite Test centre having taken 0–119 the last time I bowled there.

They'd had an Elvis Presley evening, something I'd shared with Bob and John as a Presley fan, when we often played his tapes on quiet evenings in India and Pakistan. The fact that they had taken the trouble to drop a line to Deadly, their old team mate, made me realize that there was not necessarily direct animosity against me, more against what WSC stood for.

It must have been at the Cornhill reception for us on the way to the airport that I first began to relax, discovering that other members of the team had all the usual problems associated with getting ready to go off on tour and I began to feel part of the England set-up once more.

Everybody appeared rather suspicious of the tour. We were amazed that the management hadn't even received playing conditions on the day we left. That confirmed the lack of co-ordination between the two boards of control. We felt we were going into the unknown having accepted an incredible itinerary in terms of matches and flights around Australia.

It meant the management had virtually to settle on the Test side before we left and this would never have been the case on a more traditional tour, where players would vie for places in the Test team.

I was just so grateful to be back on an England tour that I didn't worry about being left out of the first four-day game against Queensland and I reckoned that as I'd had experience of so much cricket in Australia it made sense for the newer men to have a work-out in unfamiliar conditions.

I still put in my stint at the nets in Brisbane during the game against Queensland and for my efforts, finished up by smashing my head open on a board that was jutting out as I walked back with Ken Barrington. Derek Randall (Arkle) batted with typical improvisation for his 97 on a wicket that made stroke playing a risky business.

My first taste of cricket with England again came at Newcastle and getting some wickets and being named Man of the Match in one of the one-day games against Northern New South Wales did my confidence no end of good.

WSC reared its head once more in several passing conversations while we were there. Several people, including cricket officials, kept coming up to me and saying such things as, 'Welcome back, it's nice to see you back, playing real cricket.' I kept thinking 'What on earth do they think I've been playing out here for the past two winters?' They obviously regarded WSC games as a joke or as a circus and, in the country areas, didn't appear to have understood just how competitive that cricket was. I answered them politely and realized they had barely understood how tough and real WSC had been, ironically far more so than the one-day games we played in Newcastle!

We went to Adelaide, taking on the Combined Universities in the odd circumstances of being engaged in a four-day match, which wasn't even first-class. This was hardly the right preparation for the Tests against Australia.

Selfishly, I suppose, it was good for me because I finished up with 8 for 41, a ludicrous figure on such a good Adelaide wicket. I relied on bowling a good line against players who did not possess as good a defensive technique as normal first-class players. I was helped too by some excellent close catching. With a bit of drift, bowling a little slower and putting the field back, we had them holing-out at cover and mid-on in the latter stages. Suddenly I realized this was my best analysis ever for England and thought, someone up there is favouring me and must have been saying, 'Well, I wanted you back!'

It meant a great deal to me when Mike Brearley asked me to lead the team off the field, saying, 'Well bowled, Deadly, it's good to have you back.' I knew he meant it and replied, 'It's nice to be back.'

It doesn't matter whether it's an English cricketing season or a tour, but every player needs a good performance early on. One desperately wants wickets or runs at an early stage.

It went even better for me in Tasmania. Because of the extraordinary weather we had experienced during the English season – I can remember play being stopped for snow, sleet, hail, fog and sea mists or frost – but until we reached Hobart on this tour I'd never known a first-class match stopped by the wind! We encountered gales that were timed at ninety miles per hour. The bails hardly ever stayed on and the batsmen literally struggled to stay on their feet when taking strike. Sudden gusts made life hazardous for the bowlers too. In the end, on the second day, the appeal of the Tasmanian batsmen was upheld by the umpires and we lost about half a day's play.

I had the ridiculous analysis of 3 for 13 in 10 overs. To allow for the wind I was aiming the ball in the direction of second slip and seeing it blown back somewhere near the batsman. Graham Gooch and David Gower (Lulu) batted with such ferocity in our second innings that we were able to declare and Tasmania responded by having a go for victory on the final afternoon.

Brian Davison, the Rhodesian all-rounder, who plays for Leicestershire, and captains Tasmania in the winter, was an important man for us to get rid of quickly. Before he could get going we got him lbw off the best ball I had bowled at that stage of the tour.

New Zealand fast bowler, Richard Hadlee, another star man signed by Tasmania, fought through the last 20 overs but with Geoff Miller's support we finished the game off in the best possible way when I had him caught at slip off the last ball of the game.

The cold tubes, as the Australians refer to their cans of beer, tasted even more refreshing that evening when our scorer, Geoffrey Saulez, went through my match analysis of 10 for 77. The only upsetting feature of our visit to Tasmania was the premature departure from the tour of Derbyshire's 'Mr Reliable', Mike Hendrick. Hendo had worked like smoke to clear up his shoulder trouble and we'd all spent time trying to help him in the nets at Brisbane. Bernard Thomas, the team's travelling physiotherapist and injury expert, had done everything possible to keep Mike with us, but in the end he was forced to accept that he could not bowl effectively and had to return home from Melbourne the day we left Tasmania, just a month after leaving England.

There was an extra sadness as we sat trying to cheer Mike up over a few beers in the Wrest Point Casino Hotel, one of the best we stayed in throughout the tour. Everyone knew how much his accurate bowling would be missed in both the one-day internationals and Tests, especially after the magnificent job he had done there a year ago. There are few more heartfelt sporting moments than when a player has to return home injured in the middle of a tour.

Alec Bedser announced that Yorkshire's up-and-coming young seamer, Graham Stevenson, would be flying out to replace him.

3. The White Ball and Other Innovations

The wrangling about the white ball, coloured clothing and the use of circles on the pitch went on for almost three weeks at the start of the tour. Alec Bedser, and Brearley, along with the chairman of the TCCB, George Mann, had a series of discussions with the Australian Cricket Board and PBL, Kerry Packer's company, which had won the contract to market the game in Australia over the next ten years.

One of the main arguments surrounding the white ball was whether it should be used for all World Series Cup games or simply for the night matches being staged at the Sydney Cricket Ground.

On the coach journey from Newcastle down to Sydney, Mike Brearley canvassed the opinions of the team and we came up with a 14–2 vote against using the white ball outside night cricket. Everyone accepted that it was necessary for the matches being played under the brilliant lighting system in Sydney. From England's point of view I was the only player who'd had experience of the white ball, playing floodlit cricket, and using the circles.

The management consulted me for my opinions about night cricket before we left England, and I got the impression that the attitude of Lord's was that they were not prepared to accept all the demands of the Australian Board wholesale regarding the triangular tournament between England, Australia and the West Indies. Who could blame them for this stance, because they had no experience of the conditions surrounding night cricket.

The Australians, for instance, put forward a suggestion for different balls to be used at each end during night games. Their case was that the white ball tended to become discoloured quickly, but we could see this system helping their barrage of quick bowlers and we thought we would be at a disadvantage because we relied a good deal more on slow bowlers. So after more negotiations this idea was discarded.

All three countries agreed that they could claim one refurbished ball after 25 overs during the innings and although the white ball did tend to go a slightly yellowish colour towards the end of 50 overs a different ball was hardly ever called for. Spectators and television audiences did occasionally find it difficult to pick up the ball at the end of an innings.

I could understand some of our players and the management being a bit suspicious or apprehensive about the white ball after playing cricket at home for years with the traditional red ball. My attitude before we embarked on the night games was not to sing the praises too much about this unique version of international cricket and I did not want to conjure up problems for my team-mates. I said to them, 'Play it and then judge for yourselves.'

Batsmen like Graham Gooch, Peter Willey and David Gower were immediately impressed and our only initial problems seemed to be complaints by those who were fielding square on either side of the wicket, and of the wicketkeeper and slipfielders.

There were a few teething troubles catching the white ball – it seemed to come at us a bit quicker at night and we found it harder on the hands than the conventional red one. I remember a ball the West Indian all-rounder Collis King received breaking the skin and drawing blood, which was due to the seam standing out more sharply on this type of ball.

The red and white balls have tended to have smaller seams in Australia this year than in the past. This reduced some of the effectiveness of the fast bowlers as they were not able to swing it about quite as much or acquire as much bounce as they did with the type of balls used in the 1960s and 1970s.

The players realized the assistance of picking up the white ball against coloured clothing. But, again, our cricketing authorities were not prepared to forsake the traditional white shirts and white flannels worn by England teams over the years, probably because they saw it as commercial exploitation.

The Australians and the West Indians settled for wearing shirts and flannels that had their colours in stripes down the side of their shirts, trousers and around the collar. These were totally inadequate for the needs of night cricket compared with the coloured clothing we had worn for WSC games. Then, from the point of view of the players, spectators and television audiences, the pastel shades of powder-blue worn by the World, canary-yellow worn by Australia, and cherry-pink adopted by the West Indies were a success.

The West Indians did not like what they called their 'poofter pink' apparel and thought that khaki or fawn would have been a more suitable colour. I'm sure England would have looked smart in, say, a royal blue outfit which would have shown off the white ball admirably.

Our compromise was to settle for dark-blue-cum-black pads and batting gloves which everyone adjusted to quickly after initially thinking they looked rather strange.

To a certain extent, I could understand our management declining to go along with so many radical changes all at once, so we insisted on our normal white clothing, but I am sure that the next time such a series is staged in Australia we will agree for England to play in coloured clothing.

Without doubt, Kerry Packer's most dramatic and most successful innovation was the launching of night cricket. England players got into their stride quickly and appreciated what a tremendous spectacle the night matches were for the public. The six mighty pylons soaring into the sky lit up the arena so well that England cricketers were even admitting the light was better than they often encountered on grey, gloomy days back home. For the spectator in the stand or on the Hill or for ourselves sitting in the dressing-room, we wouldn't have known whether it was night or day if you looked straight out below the level of the skyline. Perhaps the pylons are something of an eyesore during day-time and it's a shame a system used in baseball stadiums in Japan, where similar lights are lifted hydraulically, was not considered. The England team were also astonished that there were no problems with shadows.

In time, I can see the lights being installed at the Adelaide Oval and at Melbourne. In Melbourne they could possibly build in a lighting system on the lines of the lights that were inserted along the top of the stands at Victoria Football League Park where we played our W S C night games in that city. There is such a committed following for the game in Victoria that I could easily see crowds of forty to fifty thousand flocking to night cricket at the Melbourne Cricket Ground. If the money could be raised, night games must surely spread to India and the West Indies where they have an ideal climate and a ready-made public to support this type of international cricket.

One of the most obvious attractions of the night matches was that the general public were able to do at least half a day's work and even a full day at the office or in the factory and still see four or five hours of the match. It has always seemed sad to me that so much professional cricket around the world has been played when most people cannot get to the grounds.

I would even advocate a sliding scale of charges at the turnstile so that a stand ticket would cost the full price at the start and slightly less for those who arrive between innings or when night play has started.

Night cricket obviously appeals to a new cricketing audience because very few of the Sydney Cricket Ground's membership of fifteen thousand bothered to attend, yet the night matches drew regular attendances of over fifteen thousand regardless of whether Australia were involved or even in the running for a place in the World Series finals.

From the crowd point of view, watching at night was so much more comfortable than roasting in temperatures of anything from 80° to 100°F at the height of the day. The balmy summer evenings in Sydney were ideal for watching, and perfect weather in which to play. This brought me to wondering whether it would be feasible to experiment with night matches in England. After all, there are quite a number of occasions when, because of daylight lasting in midsummer, we could probably carry on playing until, say, 9 p.m. But how warm would it be in June or July? And would the playing conditions be awkward because of the heavy dew we get on the ground even in a good summer? I still think our cricketing authorities should look at the possibility of night cricket for some one-day competitions, maybe finding the right sponsor or working on a fund-raising scheme to install lights at one major cricketing centre, perhaps Nottingham, Leeds, Manchester or London.

It is obvious that the public in Australia have taken to the night game and if it is going to help international cricket remain solvent, all other Test-playing countries should examine cricket under floodlights. It cannot be too far off when Test cricket is tried out at night and with a white ball, even if the traditionalists throw up their hands in horror at the suggestion. I regard night cricket as the forerunner to more indoor cricket, which is becoming increasingly popular in England.

I also think that it won't be long before we see coloured bats being used at night in the professional games with countries adopting different colours for the bats they use in Tests. Graham Roope, the Surrey and England batsman, used a blue bat in a few first-class matches on behalf of Slazenger but it was banned by the TCCB who regarded it as gimmicky.

England were understandably adamant about not using the circles which were an accepted part of one-day cricket with WSC.

The West Indians and most of the Australians were familiar with the circles and they would have had an advantage had we given way to the requests of the Australian Board and the sponsors who wanted to use them.

Basically, the system of circles was designed to encourage a more normal type of cricket in the limited-overs game. Originally, two circles were drawn at both ends of a thirty-yard radius, taking the middle stump as the centre.

The circles did not encroach on the area of the wicket and were intended as a line inside which a minimum number of fielders had to be placed.

The rule was that for the first 15 overs of a 50-over match no more than two players, excluding the bowler and wicket-keeper, could be outside the circles at the moment of delivery. Two fielders during those 15 overs had to be in catching positions and this situation was assessed by the umpires. For the remaining overs not more than five players could be outside the circles at the moment of delivery. 'No ball' would be called or a fielder would be sharply warned by the umpire if he was not inside the circle when the ball was delivered. There was a definite incentive for batsmen to have a go and try to pick up extra runs against such attacking fields. This scheme might work against the interests of the spinners whom it would be difficult to bring on in the first 15 overs. Imagine John Emburey trying to bowl to a field with only two men out!

This ruling was good in that it prevented captains from putting six or seven men right back on the fence and letting the batsman pick up ones and twos.

In our last two games against the West Indies it looked wrong when bowlers of the calibre of Andy Roberts and Michael Holding had six or seven men back, content to let singles be scored. The crowds would have had far better value and seen more action, more runs and more running by the fielders, with the restrictions imposed by the circles.

Mike Brearley came in for heavy criticism from the Australian media and Australian crowds, especially at Sydney in our first night encounter when we beat the West Indies in a hair-raising last ball finish. Even wicketkeeper David Bairstow was standing just a few feet from the sightscreen, with everyone else spread around the boundary fence. These were legitimate tactics but could never happen under the circles system.

Tony Greig pointed out that the circles produced a more genuine form of the game because batsmen were able to carry on playing orthodox attacking shots instead of being forced to improvise in an effort to beat totally defensive field settings. That must be good for the players and for cricket fans.

We also proved that with more men forced to stand in attacking fielding positions we had scores nearer the 250 and 260 mark instead of around 200. So the public were seeing more boundaries and perhaps getting 60 or 70 runs more in every one-day game, another argument for the circles.

One of Australia's latest ideas, and a sensible one, is for semicircles to be drawn in an arc behind the stumps to run round to square leg on one side and to where point would normally be on the other side. The most likely suggestion to be adopted is one circle drawn in the shape of the oval with its centre point the middle of the wicket.

These would be the guidelines for the future system of one-day matches. People might think that a series of circles on the ground would be unsightly. We found that spectators at ground level couldn't see them anyway and those sitting up in the stands grew to appreciate the entertainment value of this innovation which, incidentally, has been used for years in South African cricket and according to players like Barry Richards, Mike

Procter and Graeme Pollock, has been an unqualified success in their country.

I'm sure that the TCCB will see the light regarding circles and at least experiment with them in one or other of our three one-day domestic competitions. They must be for the good of limited-overs cricket and the Australians are determined they will use them for all future one-day international matches.

4. The First Test

Considering I was about to play in my 75th Test match for England I was in an unusually apprehensive state before the series got under way against Australia in Perth.

A combination of reasons made me anxious about this Test. I was obviously concerned about how it would go after being out of the Test side for over two years and the build-up to the First Test had been anything but ideal for all of us. Also I had never bowled a ball at the Western Australian Cricket Association ground despite going there under three different England captains – Ray Illingworth in 1970–71, Mike Denness in 1974–5 and Tony Greig in 1977. The nearest I had come to bowling at the Perth ground was appearing across the road at Gloucester Park in WSC.

When we got to Perth I was quite prepared to hear that I was not going to play. This ground has always assisted the faster bowlers and Test teams have tended to go for the extra seamer there. When England had played a Test in Perth the previous season, John Lever had been included and had taken important wickets, and I could see a strong case for his being selected again.

Uneasiness ran through the team because we'd had no experience of playing at Perth on this tour. We wondered, in fact, if we weren't the first major touring side to go into a Test without having the benefit of playing a first-class game beforehand at this venue. Our fears were increased as the Perth wicket over the years has had the reputation of being one of the quickest in the world.

We were also conscious that we were entering the First Test

just after having had a concentrated period of one-day cricket in Sydney. That type of cricket is anything but ideal for bowlers wanting to have some rhythm and long spells behind them. The demands of bowling in one-day games are also so different from the approach to Test matches.

There was an unusual amount of debate about the likely format of our Test line-up, Mike Hendrick having gone home early because of his shoulder injury.

Bob Willis had desperately been looking for an extra yard of pace on the tour and although Graham Dilley was clearly going to get his chance he'd never experienced a full day in the field in his life. Now he was going to be pitched into Test cricket where he might find himself in the field for a day and a half or three days out of the five.

With big Bob seeming to have lost a certain amount of edge, we realized it would be an almighty onus on Ian Botham to get out there and bowl more overs than we should expect from a player of even his incredible stamina.

The assortment of selection headaches must have led to an extra long meeting among the selectors who were the manager, Alec Bedser, his assistant, Ken Barrington; Mike Brearley, the captain; Bob Willis, the vice-captain and Ian Botham, with Bernard Thomas, physiotherapist and medical specialist sitting in to give up-to-date information on any fitness doubts.

It's so much easier to tell England players whether or not they have been chosen for a Test when they are on tour. On this occasion Mike Brearley simply said that those who wanted to know the team could come to the team room at such and such a time.

It made me think back to the occasion in England when I was fielding near the boundary in a John Player match and a spectator beckoned me saying, 'Bad luck.' To be told by a spectator is not the nicest way to hear one has been dropped from the England side.

It has always seemed wrong that the media and the public get to hear who is playing for England before the players themselves are informed. Perhaps a system could be devised whereby a Test team can be chosen on a Thursday or Friday for games at home, with players being notified by the selectors or the captain before the side is released to the media.

For instance, I discovered I'd been left out of the MCC tour to the West Indies in 1967–8 when I heard it on my car radio as I was driving to Dover to play for Kent. Being left out of a Test at home is much harder to take than when you are part of a tour. It's extremely hard for the young player who has had only a slight taste of Test cricket if he hears through a radio announcement that he has been dropped. There's that feeling that you've got to go back to your county and start all over again to prove that you're a Test cricketer. On tour you are still an integral part of the party and will still be in the reckoning for later Tests because the selection is restricted to a group of sixteen or seventeen players.

On this occasion in Perth, the captain made a point of coming to me at the swimming-pool and congratulated me on returning to the England XI.

I supposed I'd got my place because I'd been lucky enough to pick up wickets in Adelaide and Hobart but what worried me was when I analysed what I'd done at that stage I realized I had never bowled against a Test player in a four-day match.

There is such a gulf between the county or state player and the fully-fledged Test cricketer. It made it difficult to assess whether I was bowling that well or whether I'd been flattered by being England's leading wicket-taker at that point of the tour.

As though I didn't have enough things on my mind on the eve of my Test come-back, I had an injury in the nets when a ball, hit in slip catching practice flicked the end of my left index finger.

Ironically, it was the first ball that had been hit to me. My finger swelled up painfully and it couldn't have happened to a worse part of my hand from the point of view of my bowling grip. I made light of my injury for obvious reasons. I wasn't going to miss out on playing for England again!

My part in the slip-fielding rehearsal had come about because our expert slip formation had been broken up with Hendo going home and Gooch being dropped. It meant we went into the Test with virtually only one expert in this position, Mike Brearley, although Geoff Miller is an accomplished catcher in this area.

I heard criticism about the 'imbalance' of our attack because it contained three spinners, but one had to appreciate that Peter Willey had played impressively as a batsman and was largely in the side on this strength, while Miller had been a major success with his off-spinners in Australia the year before.

Derek Randall deserved to be opening because he had looked to be the second best player to Boycott. There was a feeling it would have been nicer to have opened the series at, say, Adelaide rather than at Perth, as we viewed the prospect of Jeff Thomson and Dennis Lillee being back in harness against us for the first time in four years with apprehension. We really expected to find ourselves on the quickest wicket in Australia.

We could not have wished for a better start because after winning the toss Brearley had the pleasure of seeing the Australians struggling at 20 for 3, mainly because of the magnificent bowling performance by Botham. If we'd had Hendo at the other end, we would have made greater inroads as the ball seamed and bounced on a wicket that had patches of green and dampness throughout.

When I was brought into the attack I was pretty nervous and didn't bowl particularly well, trying to allow for the drift which comes with the famous wind, the Fremantle Doctor, which blows across the WACA. Probably one of the worst balls I delivered in the series denied Kim Hughes his 100. Brearley had just moved himself to square leg, making it an extra man on the on side. Hughes hit it fairly hard and Brearley did well to hold on to a catch above his head. Hughes walked away understandably crestfallen about getting out at 99 to that particular delivery. Bob Willis was terribly unlucky beating the bat so often but not getting wickets.

I was delighted to share in Graham Dilley's first Test wicket by holding on to a catch around my ankles down at long leg which disposed of Peter Toohey. Dill had done a good job, too, in supporting Botham's Herculean and seemingly endless spells at the other end which included an amazing stretch in which he bowled throughout a session in the blazing heat.

We could not have got off to a worse start with the bat, Lillee bagging Boycott and Randall both for nought, Hughes holding an astonishing slip catch almost off his right toe-cap to dismiss the latter, who could only stare in disbelief as the Australians ran to mob Hughes. The captain and young Dilley prevented the Australians from taking complete hold of the Test on the second day in a brave seventh-wicket partnership and it said a lot for Dilley's temperament at the age of only twenty. He could never have faced such class fast bowling yet he displayed a classic defence knowing just when to get his bat out of the way. His example should have been a lesson for us all and there was certainly a feeling in the dressing-room that if Dill could do it then our recognized batsmen should have been able to put us in a much stronger position.

It must have been especially satisfying for the captain; he had suffered all kinds of criticism and abuse from the Australian media and public, who argued that he was not good enough to be in the side even if his captaincy was beyond reproach. He played Lillee, Thomson, and Dymock as well as anybody for his 64.

This Test threw up two perfect examples to vindicate the cause of the crash helmet. There has been a bit of a lobby in English Cricket to outlaw the wearing of helmets in the field, yet if Willey had not had the protection of one when fielding at short leg in Australia's second innings, he would have been severely injured.

Back at the hotel that evening Willey announced that he thought his helmet had 'saved his life' and even then, the ball had struck him so hard on the side of the helmet that he needed stitches in a wound behind his ear. On previous occasions during the tour we'd more than realized the value of helmets as several times people had been hit in the head by lifting deliveries. The spinners appreciated them because we relied on men fielding in close catching positions when the ball is turning and there's a huge risk for anyone standing too closely to the bat.

The most popular type of helmet is the one that protects the temples and ears without any perspex visor or grille covering the face. If Alan Border had been wearing that kind of helmet during his heroic second innings century he would have been saved from bruising and cuts when caught by a lifting delivery from Dilley as he went to hook.

In WSC almost everyone wore varying types of protective headwear and in the last of those Super-Tests against Lillee and Co., it undoubtedly helped me to get 30 in a tail-end partnership with Garth Le Roux.

From my point of view the helmet has certainly helped when batting. My nerve had not been good ever since a lightning delivery from Michael Holding came dangerously close to finishing my career during the Old Trafford Test against the West Indies in 1976.

With the added confidence of a helmet I found it easier to get behind the line of the ball against the extra-fast bowlers. Without a helmet you tend to be thinking more often than not, there's one coming in a minute. For someone like myself, if I've just been fortunate enough to have edged a boundary the fast bowler is likely to come charging in to let me know he's the boss and I'm sure it plays much more on a batsman's mind if he hasn't got a helmet on. It's easier to say to yourself, I'll get behind it if he lets me have a bouncer. My reaction is not to duck against the bouncer because my reflexes are not that quick. It means I'm a more vulnerable target.

Even class players like Barry Richards wore them playing with WSC and I saw him pinned twice. The great Viv Richards, Barry's West Indian namesake, still declined to wear a helmet and even a player of his genius came perilously close to being hit on the head as balls flicked his cap a couple of times.

Helmets must make sense when two of the world's greatest batsmen can come so close to being hurt. South African Keppler Wessels, who plays for Sussex and Queensland, is an interesting case. He is a marvellous player but is someone who likes to get on the front foot. I have seen him hit seven times on the helmet and before this kind of protection came in I'm sure he would have sustained an injury which could have severely affected his career. Helmets are almost compulsory when facing the West Indies in recent years, because they come at you with four of the fastest bowlers in the world and gone are the days when one got some respite from fast bowling.

There's another aspect too in the case for helmets: the public surely gets better value out of seeing more batsmen prepared to take on the fast bowlers either trying to pull or hook them when they dig it in short.

Fatalities in cricket are becoming more common and we were all appalled on hearing that two boys aged twelve and eight were killed playing local cricket in Melbourne whilst we were there for the final Test. They were both struck on the head and we wondered whether their lives wouldn't have been saved if they'd had the benefit of crash helmets.

Chest-protectors have also become fashionable in the Test arena and it is not uncommon to see some batsmen allowing the ball to rear up into their rib cage rather than risk getting an edge and so feeding those short legs who lurk round the corner.

Sunil Gavaskar and one or two other Indian batsmen tried another innovation, wearing plastic shields over the forearm in the Tests against England last summer, and why not, if it's going to mean preventing a fractured bone that would put a batsman out of the game for weeks?

Sadly, the second day of the Perth Test will always be remembered for Lillee's histrionics with his aluminium bat. I had a close-up view of the proceedings that led to one of the strangest hold-ups I've ever seen in a Test match. We had seen Dennis carrying his aluminium bat and when he hit the ball towards extra cover there was a sound like the ringing of a church bell. We were certain that if he'd played the same shot with a conventional willow bat it would have gone for four. At the end of the over I was setting off for third man when the arguments about Dennis's infamous bat started with Brearley querying its use.

The umpires were uncertain whether Dennis should be allowed to carry on after Brearley had complained that there were clear scuff marks on the ball as a result of contact with the aluminium face. Lillee insisted he was within his rights to use it, saying that the Australian Cricket Board had not refused him permission to play with it. He had used it without any success in the previous test against the West Indies in Brisbane and no one had made a fuss.

But what was sad about this unnecessary episode in a Test match was Dennis's extraordinary display when his captain, Greg Chappell, emerged from the pavilion carrying two more bats in an effort to sort out the dispute which held up the game for almost ten minutes. Dennis hurled his tin bat some twenty yards, clearly infuriated by Chappell's orders to use a normal bat. I thought it was a pity to see perhaps the greatest fast bowler in the history of the game behaving in such a way. This was a shocking example for hundreds of adoring young cricket lovers who regard Lillee as their idol, particularly in Western Australia, where he can do nothing wrong.

The whole incident showed a lack of respect for the umpires, who were in an understandable state of confusion as they were not sure whether Dennis was within his rights using the aluminium bat. Lillee showed no remorse about the unsavoury interruption of a Test match, and it is apparently a sign of weakness for an Australian Test cricketer to apologize or in any way regret such acts of misconduct on the field.

After that day's play I talked to Dennis about his aluminium bat and he stressed that it was an excellent investment for schools and for young players because here was a bat that was being marketed to last for ever. Dennis had clearly seen the situation as an outstanding piece of sales promotion around the world!

Our later-order batsmen, taking their cue from Brearley and Dilley, grafted well enough to reduce Australia's first-innings lead to the slender margin of 16 runs. But we had lost our grip once more, with Julien Wiener and Bruce Laird playing soundly and putting on 91 in their opening partnership of the second innings.

I broke up their stand and had men up around the bat, which neither of them liked. We used a silly mid-off against Wiener, who seemed to push forward a lot with his pad. He came down the wicket and hit me straight over the top for six, part of his tactics to get rid of the close-to-the-wicket fielders. But our plans worked; Randall, wearing a helmet, clutched a thick inside edge in the bat-pad position. That night, however, Australia had reached 168 for 2, and the game had definitely swung their way.

The next morning it was gratifying for me to have Greg Chappell stumped; he was lured down the wicket by my slower ball. But we still had to contend with the left-hander Alan

Border, who had fought his way into a side that had threatened to be dominated by men who had been involved with WSC, although the balance was only 6/5 in their favour for the First Test at Perth.

Border had done well in India against their spinners a few weeks earlier, and played me confidently. I found he was a very strong off-side player and tried to bowl straight or in at his legs but he still made room, forcing me through extra cover. Lillee blocked so well, giving Border the strike, that we could see this Test slipping away. Border's 106 was immensely important to Australia because his innings occupied extra time and gave us no chance of possibly having a day and a half in which to pursue a score of about 320. Instead, our target was 354 and we felt that victory was beyond us. It was going to be more a case of having a day and thirty-five minutes to last out for a draw.

Botham had not been quite so effective with the new ball the second time around, but came back to finish off the Australians 5 for 98 and ended up with the remarkable match analysis of 11 for 176.

Being realistic, we saw we weren't going to win this Test but we were confident about being able to bat it out for a draw even though we'd lost Randall overnight in bad light which had led to an early close. As it was, Boycott batted throughout and showed us all that with sound technique and application this match should have been saved. We had to admire the way Geoff fought it out, finishing one run short of his century and becoming the only man to carry his bat for 99 in a Test, as well as joining Len Hutton and Bobby Abel as the only English batsman who have carried their bat in Tests against Australia. It was sad that he was deprived of a century in his come-back against the combination of Lillee and Thomson after critics had accused him of not being good enough to score runs against bowlers of their calibre.

What it needed was for one recognized batsman to stay with Geoff for a session. Botham hung on for sixty-eight minutes,

Dilley for fifty-seven and Bob Taylor for fifty-two but nobody stayed for quite long enough. Someone really needed to be at the other end for an hour and a half with him. There was some rather loose batting considering that the name of our game should have been survival, and our defence had been poor. Even when I came in during the last 20 overs I worked out that Geoff ought to be able to take about 12 overs, leaving me to play something like 48 deliveries.

Unfortunately, one of my principal batting deficiencies was severely exposed at the wrong moment. My problem is not being quite sure where my off stump is, something that's so commendable about Dilley's batting technique. It means I'm inclined to play at balls wide of the off stump which I should be leaving well alone.

I was one of Geoff Dymock's six victims and he did really well with the new ball, moving it across the right-handers and getting the odd one to swing back. From our point of view it was good to see Botham being named for the $1,000 Man of the Match award after his superhuman efforts with the ball. Dilley too had bowled accurately in his first Test and had the satisfaction of a dismissal that titillated the scorers, the book reading 'Lillee caught Willey bowled Dilley' in the second innings. My personal reflections of my first Test since my departure to WSC was that I had bowled far better in the second innings, in which I'd got their first three men out on a wicket that did not offer much for the spinners.

Although dressing-room morale was still high after losing the match, we all thought we were good enough to have come away from Perth with a draw instead of going to Sydney one down. The Australians had lost the toss but had shown themselves to be the better equipped side, and when I recall the downcast atmosphere of the England dressing-room after previous defeats the situation here was very different. There had been an enthusiasm and bubble about this team with everyone encouraging one another in the dressing-room and out on the field. The bowlers were being lifted all the time and this was a big spur for a youngster like Dilley.

We were obviously disappointed with our performance and realized how hard it was to get back into a three-match series when the first one has gone wrong. Most of the England players had become accustomed to success in the past couple of years and this could have had an adverse reaction, but the feeling was that we were good enough to win at Sydney or Melbourne, wickets where the ball might turn a little. We also fancied our chances in the one-day internationals.

The most pertinent lesson to come out of this defeat, when we sat down and talked about what had gone wrong, was the way Boycott and Brearley had batted. Aged thirty-eight and thirty-seven they were easily our most senior players, and perhaps it was significant that they had survived far more successfully than the younger brigade who are now reared on a domestic cricket programme so much geared to limited-overs competitions. Boycott and Brearley had both had more chances of learning how to build a long innings and showed the vital asset of a sound defensive technique. We also thought it perverse that the fast bowlers we had talked about most did not play such a crucial part in our downfall. Rodney Hogg, the scourge of England in the winter of 1978 dropped out of this Test because of injury, and Lillee and Thomson had not turned out to be as lethal a partnership as we had anticipated. Instead, Australia's veteran Dymock, at the age of thirty-four, turned out to be their match winner. England had respected him in the past but never guessed he would be cast in the rôle of the destroyer at Perth after his belated arrival into Test cricket.

1st TEST v. AUSTRALIA

Played at Perth, 14–19 December 1979. **Australia won by 138 runs.**

AUSTRALIA

Batsman	First innings		Second innings	
J. M. Wiener	run out	11	c Randall b Underwood	58
B. M. Laird	lbw b Botham	0	c Taylor b Underwood	33
A. R. Border	lbw b Botham	4	c Taylor b Willis	115
*G. S. Chappell	c Boycott b Botham	19	st Taylor b Underwood	43
K. J. Hughes	c Brearley b Underwood	99	c Miller b Botham	4
P. M. Toohey	c Underwood b Dilley	19	c Taylor b Botham	3
†R. W. Marsh	c Taylor b Dilley	42	c Gower b Botham	4
R. J. Bright	c Taylor b Botham	17	lbw b Botham	12
D. K. Lillee	c Taylor b Botham	18	c Willey b Dilley	19
G. Dymock	b Botham	5	not out	20
J. R. Thomson	not out	1	b Botham	8
Extras	(B4 LB3 NB2)	9	(B4 LB5 W2 NB7)	18
Total		244		337

Fall of wickets: 1–2, 2–17, 3–20, 4–88, 5–127, 6–186, 7–219, 8–219, 9–243, 10–244.

1–91, 2–100, 3–168, 4–183, 5–191, 6–204, 7–225, 8–303, 9–323, 10–337.

ENGLAND

Batsman	First innings		Second innings	
D. W. Randall	c Hughes b Lillee	0	lbw b Dymock	1
G. Boycott	lbw b Lillee	0	not out	99
P. Willey	c Chappell b Dymock	9	lbw b Dymock	12
D. I. Gower	c Marsh b Lillee	17	c Thomson b Dymock	23
G. Miller	c Hughes b Thomson	25	c Chappell b Thomson	8
*J. M. Brearley	c Marsh b Lillee	64	(7) c Marsh b Bright	11
I. T. Botham	c Toohey b Thomson	15	(6) c Marsh b Lillee	18
†R. W. Taylor	b Chappell	14	b Lillee	15
G. R. Dilley	not out	38	c Marsh b Dymock	16
D. L. Underwood	lbw b Dymock	13	c Wiener b Dymock	0
R. G. D. Willis	b Dymock	11	c Chappell b Dymock	0
Extras	(LB7 NB15)	22	(LB3 W1 NB8)	12
Total		228		215

Fall of wickets: 1–0, 2–12, 3–14, 4–41, 5–74, 6–90, 7–123, 8–185, 9–203, 10–228.

1–8, 2–26, 3–64, 4–75, 5–115, 6–141, 7–182, 8–211, 9–211, 10–215.

BOWLING

ENGLAND	*O*	*M*	*R*	*W*	*O*	*M*	*R*	*W*
Dilley	18	1	47	2	18	3	50	1
Botham	35	9	78	6	45.5	14	98	5
Willis	23	7	47	0	26	7	52	1
Underwood	13	4	33	1	41	14	82	3
Miller	11	2	30	0	10	0	36	0
Willey					1	0	1	0
AUSTRALIA								
Lillee	28	11	73	4	23	5	74	2
Dymock	29.1	14	52	3	17.2	4	34	6
Chappell	11	6	5	1	6	4	6	0
Thomson	21	3	70	2	11	3	30	1
Bright	1	0	6	0	23	11	30	1
Wiener					8	3	22	0
Border					2	0	7	0

5. The Second Test

The torrential rain over the New Year was to become a deciding fateful factor in the Second Test in Sydney.

Curator Athol Watkins admitted he had been caught out by the rain, confessing that the wicket had been left uncovered on New Year's Eve when all twelve members of the ground staff were off duty. By the time the covers were put on, three inches of rain had descended and with more tropical storms over the next three days Watkins had little chance to prepare a Test wicket.

His prediction that the wicket would help seamers was a classic understatement. The weather was more in keeping with what we are accustomed to in a bad English summer and we were unable to practise in the outdoor nets as they were waterlogged.

In these conditions the toss was to be of paramount importance and would probably decide the match.

When we arrived on the first morning the wicket was still drying out and the surrounds were soft. There was no chance of starting before lunch. Most of the team returned to the hotel to relax and build themselves up for the possibility of playing later.

Unlike the situation in a Test match at home wickets in Australia recover far more quickly after wet weather and we were told there was a chance of starting before tea. Being one down in the series it was much more in our interest to get play under way if at all possible, and not lose valuable time.

As it turned out it would have been a fairer contest had we waited until the second day. At our traditional eve-of-the-Test dinner Geoff Boycott had arrived with a towel wrapped around his neck, saying he couldn't turn his head. He had slipped in a bunker during a round of golf and said that it felt like the whiplash one can suffer in car accidents. He had also hurt his hand.

Geoff immediately became the popular target for a lot of leg-pulling, with the rest of the side grabbing their napkins and tying them round their necks to feign the same complaint. Geoff took it all in good spirit and we settled down to dinner and discussing our tactics for the next day.

Sadly, we had lost another important and popular member of our side, Derbyshire's Geoff Miller, whose back trouble had handicapped him in Perth. A series of examinations and tests over Christmas resulted in Geoff being advised that he should fly home for expert treatment.

We were lucky that our standby replacement, John Emburey, was literally on the spot having a winter's contract with the Saint Kilda Club in Melbourne. With Randall having had such a harrowing time against Lillee in Perth it was felt that he should move down the order and Graham Gooch (Zap) was brought back to open with Boycott after making a typically adventurous 115 in the four-day game that ended in a draw with Queensland.

The Australians made one change to their First Test squad, bringing back Ian Chappell who had been smothered in controversy from the moment we arrived in Australia. He had served a three-week suspension for swearing at an umpire whilst captaining South Australia against Tasmania and got himself into more bother with the umpires when he returned to lead his state against us at Adelaide, losing his temper in a petty argument over the umpire calling dead ball when Chappell was convinced that he had taken evasive action against a rising delivery from Ian Botham. He argued that a leg bye should have been allowed. He was so disgusted with the umpire's ruling that he threw his bat down in a fit of temper. In the same match he showed scant respect for Mike Brearley when he was batting by coming on to bowl one over with all the fielders posted on the leg side in a demonstration of disapproval about the TCCB's decision not to limit the number of leg-side fielders.

This and other confrontations with the umpires in the same match led to him being reported once more and Sir Donald Bradman chaired a special tribunal to hear the evidence. This time he got what amounted to a reprieve; he was put on probation to behave himself during a six-week suspended ban from cricket.

Conveniently, he was available for this Test and was an obvious choice ahead of Peter Toohey, who had been unconvincing at Perth. The injuries to Jeff Thomson and Rodney Hogg allowed Len Pascoe to come into their attack. Bruce Laird, the gutsy little opener, had been injured against West Indies and was replaced by Rick McCosker. Australia changed their spinner too, preferring Jim Higg's leg-breaks to Ray Bright's orthodox left-arm spin.

After batting for about twenty minutes in the nets, Boycott came back to the dressing-room to announce that because of his sore neck and a damaged little finger he did not think he should play. He felt he hadn't got sufficient mobility and freedom of movement with his neck. Our reaction was one of horror at the thought of losing our prime batsman at this stage.

Being a perfectionist, Geoff is the sort of cricketer who believes it is imperative to be a hundred per cent tuned up mentally and physically for a Test match. His argument was that he shouldn't go into such an important match anything less than totally fit and he also made the point that his 'reputation was at stake'. He felt he had a lot to prove as a result of all the criticism he had endured for staying out of Test cricket between 1974 and 1977.

He had been averaging 86 in all matches in Australia, was so far ahead of every other batsman in form, and the man most likely to make us a big century in a Test. Our feeling was that he could still do an important job if only seventy or eighty per cent fit.

The captain and his deputy, Bob Willis, were locked in earnest conversation with Geoff, trying to coax him into playing and putting it to him that all the Tour party dearly wanted him to get out there. He had batted so well that he could have made the difference to our winning or losing the Test.

In the end Geoff was virtually told by Brearley that he was playing, but as the captain went out for the toss less than ten minutes before the Test was due to start Boycott told Bob Willis that he still did not wish to play, even if the team had been announced to Chappell.

In a way I could understand Geoff's attitude but two senior members of the England team appeared to be highly incensed by his reluctance to play. I wasn't particularly involved in the dispute, but I remember some people felt he didn't want to play because the wicket was rain-affected.

There could hardly have been a more unsettling atmosphere in the dressing-room minutes before we were due to begin such a vital Test, and it didn't help when Brearley signalled that we would be batting.

Geoff was to fall in a most un-Boycott-like fashion, being bowled by Dymock when stretching forward so far that he was almost off balance. With real class players like Geoff it is rare to see them being bowled in this manner.

Gooch fought it out for almost an hour and a half but in 148 minutes cricket our innings was in ruins at 90 for 7. The wicket suited the fast bowlers and in particular, as Watkins had 'predicted', it turned out to be a paradise for someone of Dymock's type and indeed for all the Australian bowlers. Our view was that had we put Australia in they would have been in just as much trouble.

The Captain's instructions to the tail-enders was not to use up too much time the next morning and to try and get quick runs so that we could have the benefit of bowling at Australia on a drying pitch.

Graham Dilley played very well once more and with Bob Willis I managed to scrape up 25 extremely valuable runs for the last wicket.

Our bowlers, Botham, Willis and Gooch, got us back into the Test by restricting the Australians to a lead of only 22. This would have been far less but for a memorable piece of batting by Ian Chappell who had shown typical disdain for convention by appearing in the traditional baggy green Australian cap instead of the favoured crash helmet.

Judging by the reception he got from the Sydney crowd, they did not view him as the current villain of Australian cricket. In recent years I've always felt that as we had come to regard Boycott as the man who would save us in a crisis so the Australians looked upon Ian Chappell in the same light. Knowing the Australians would have the best of the wicket in the fourth innings we realized we needed a good start more than ever, and Boycott produced the form that had made him the major success of the Tour. There was not a lot he could do when a ball from Pascoe suddenly reared up as Geoff went to exploit one of his biggest strengths, the square cut. It got big on him and he hit it uppishly to McCosker in the gully.

I finished up in the nightwatchman's rôle having to hang on with the captain for thirteen minutes. Our policy was for me to be preferred for the job in these circumstances rather than Bob Taylor who nine times out of ten will contribute a more substantial innings.

I enjoy the challenge of the nightwatchman's duties. Many people forget that these embrace protecting the next man in as well as shielding the batsman at the other end for fifteen or twenty minutes, trying if possible to keep him away from the strike.

It went better than we dared hope after being 38 for 3 that evening. Next day, our tactics were not to do anything silly, not to play any rash shots but just try and see some shine off the new ball, which was only 18 overs old.

With the Australians attacking flat out they did not always post a mid-off or a mid-on so that there were gaps through which we could tick over if we got the ball on the meat of the bat. No one expected me to open up and push the score along quickly.

Mike Brearley kept me going with our between-overs chats in which we kept saying to ourselves, 'that's 3 overs of Pascoe gone or that's 2 from Lillee.' We were chiselling away and Mike was playing so calmly, even if I was out-scoring him with my thick edges wide of the slips. We talked a lot and I told him, 'I wish I could look as comfortable as you'. He helped me through a nightmarish spell against Greg Chappell who kept beating me outside the off stump.

I found Chappell as awkward as anyone and reckon I am probably better against the genuinely quick bowler when you don't have so much time to think where your left foot is or where you should be moving your other foot. Against a fast bowler it's more a matter of relying on the instinctive reflex action. Greg, with 2 for 36 in 21 overs, did the kind of job that Gooch had done so well for us.

Inevitably there were some short-pitched deliveries but, as a nightwatchman, you must expect them if you hang around. I would be cross with our fast bowlers if they didn't let one or two go against the tail-ender who takes some shifting, and after all in this innings I had come in at number five. Before the series Mike and Greg had agreed not to ban bouncers against non-recognized batsmen in these circumstances.

Mike and I felt we had done a fair job both in wearing down their bowlers and in using up almost a whole session of play. There's nothing the fielding side hates more than to see a nightwatchman staying around for this length of time.

Unfortunately the captain did not last until lunch. In some quarters he was accused of playing a loose shot but from the non-striker's end it looked quite a nasty delivery from Pascoe. It pitched outside the off stump and as there was no third man Mike was looking to deflect it over the top, a fairly common shot in Australia against the quicker bowlers but it followed him and he edged a catch to Marsh. This forced Randall to come in for a few minutes before the interval. The barrackers on the Hill revealed their more humorous side with several hundred of them mimicking the quacking noise of ducks. With previous Test scores of 0–1–0 it was hardly the noise that Derek wanted to hear.

I had been rooming with him during this Test and knew just how tense and nervous he was. He worries terribly about his form and letting down the rest of the team and it was up to me to try to help him get off the mark, which he finally did with an excellent drive through mid-wicket. He literally roared at me to run.

When I got back into the dressing-room, having survived the session, there was Botham with a cigarette saying, 'Deadly, I think you need this and I look forward to delivering the case of beer I promised as you stayed there until lunch.'

I wanted just three runs to pass my best Test score of 45 not out made against the Australians back in 1968 at Headingley.

Attempting to settle in again after lunch and trying to carry on where I'd left off I found I was even more nervous than before. Dymock managed to make one bounce and I played it quite firmly only to see Border fall over clutching the ball in his midriff at short leg. To say I was choked was an understatement but I shall never forget the standing ovation given me by the Sydney crowd as I walked back.

It really looked as though Randall was going to play one of his special innings. He has the habit of annoying fast bowlers by taking an extra long time to settle in the crease and he made Lillee stop and start his run up time and time again. So Dennis responded with his own bit of gamesmanship, keeping Derek waiting by bending down and fiddling around with his boot-laces. This interplay between the two of them backfired on Randall because it stirred Lillee into bowling even quicker.

Botham and Randall lost patience against the nagging line of Greg Chappell. Botham just could not stand being scoreless for twenty minutes after blocking in a style which is so alien to his natural approach. David Gower played an extraordinary innings, the kind of which only he is capable of playing in that England team. He played and missed an incredible amount outside the off stump but because of his temperament he did not allow these blemishes to impede him in going for shots that stamp him with that little bit of extra class. He got away with pulling because of his superb footwork and eye, and so dominated the end of our innings that his unbeaten 98 came out of a total of 132 runs scored for the last five England wickets. Towards the end he produced some amazing shots, still getting the ball to the boundary despite Greg Chappell's defensive field placings.

Like Boycott at Perth he was denied the century he so much deserved with Bob Willis joking afterwards, 'Don't find yourself at the other end with me if you're in the nineties!'

We had hoped to be setting Australia something like 260 or 270 for victory. Instead the target was 216 and we missed out on what would have been a psychological breakthrough against Wiener and McCosker. We had to make a break that evening and I was very disappointed having an lbw appeal turned down against McCosker. However when we met their players later in the Australian dressing-room for a few beers Rick said he had got a thin edge before it hit his pads and I accepted his word.

Even after the rest day we were surprised to discover there was still a little dampness in the wicket at the start of play. The odd

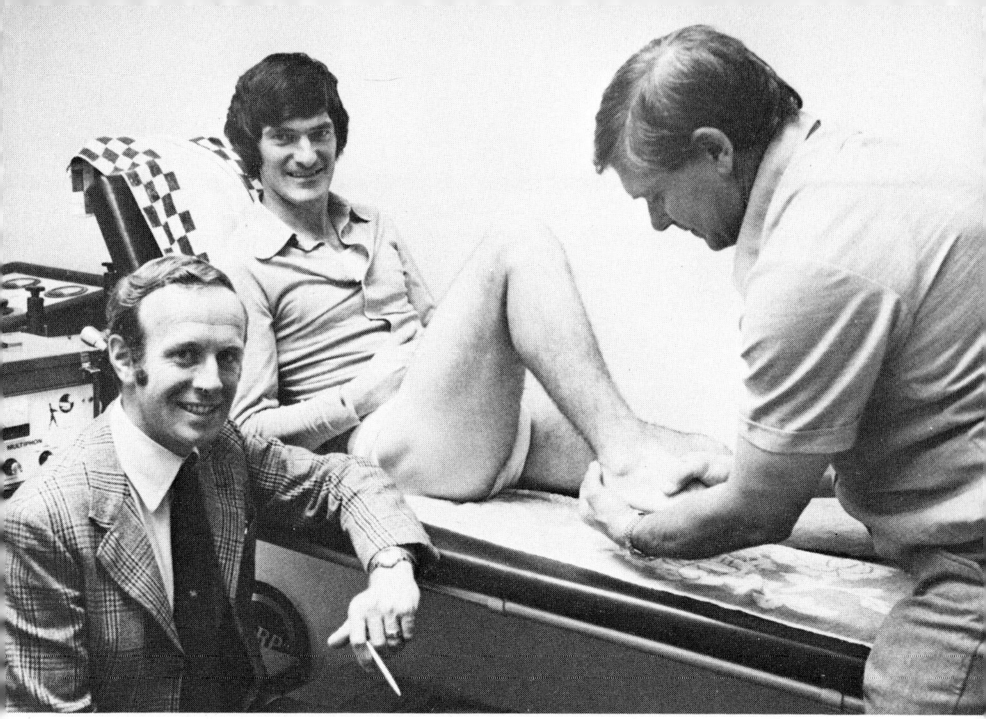

My Kent, England, and WSC team-mate wicketkeeper Alan Knott having physiotherapy.

David Bairstow and myself grinning and bearing it as Bernard Thomas puts us through one of his fitness programmes.

One of the hardest aspects of touring is being separated from one's family for up to four months. How could my wife Dawn (*left*) explain to our daughters Fiona (*below left*) and Heather (*below right*) that Daddy hadn't disappeared, and was only away in Australia playing cricket? It places a lot of pressure on wives who for various reasons cannot join their husbands for part of a tour.

Right It wasn't easy to bowl in the stifling temperatures that occur in high summer at Brisbane.

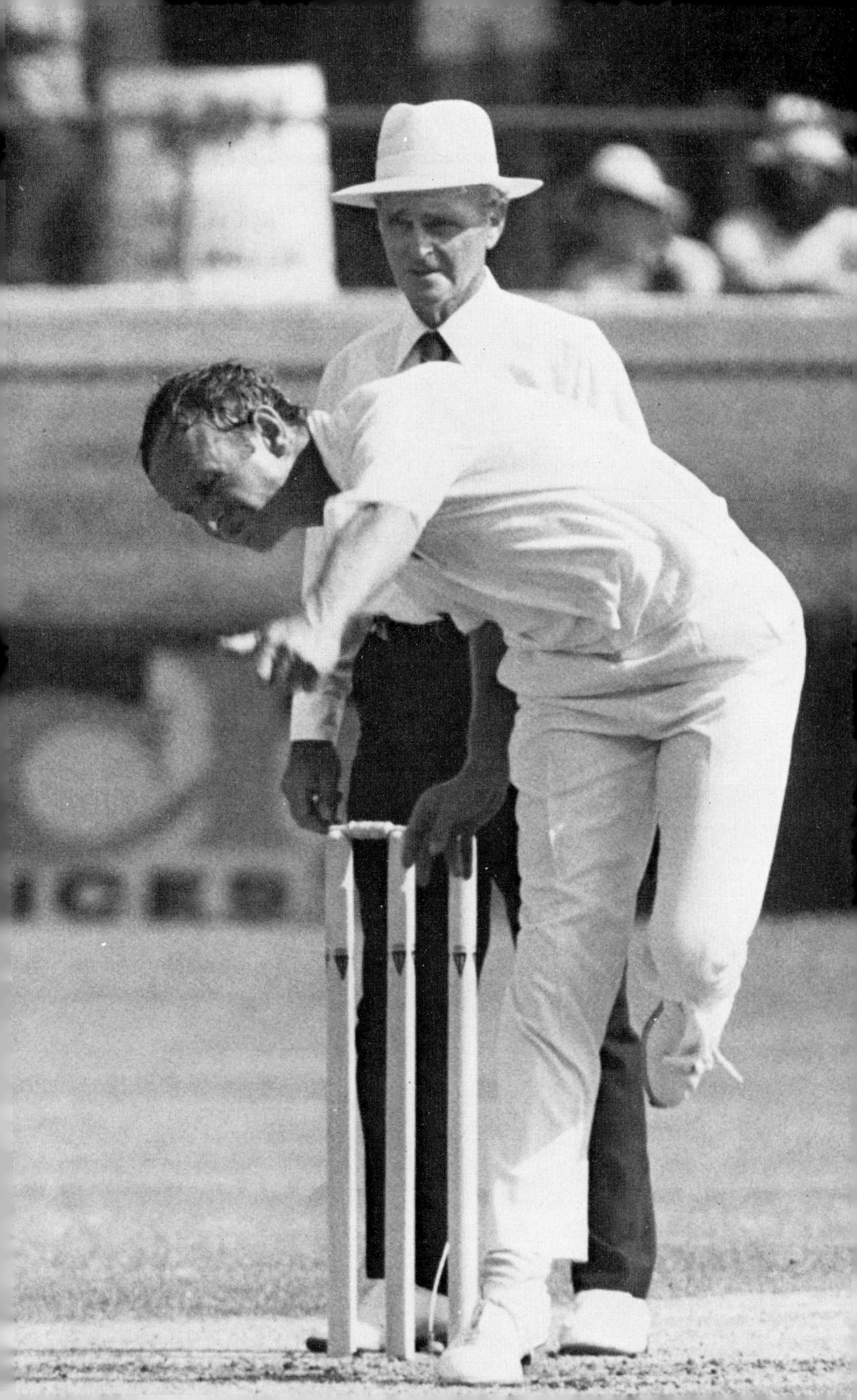

Kerry Packer and his chief WSC recruiting agent Tony Greig, appropriately seated below one of Kerry's many Channel Nine television cameras which have brought a new dimension to Australian cricket coverage.

Derek Randall just scampers home in time, the white ball cannoning into him as Victorian all-rounder Trevor Laughlin looks for the umpire's verdict. At a time when Australia were struggling to find a steady all-rounder we couldn't understand why Laughlin was shelved for the rest of the season.

In flight to Perth for the first Test match, the captain suggests he might be as quick on the draw as Clint Eastwood.

Peter Willey's audacious approach was perfectly suited for our demands, batting at no. 3 in the World Series Cup games.

The captain and one of his principal lieutenants find something to laugh about as they leave the field during the Sydney Test. Brearley and Botham have enormous respect for one another, Ian having learned so much about the finer points of captaincy from Mike, who in turn would frequently consult the Somerset 'Colossus' for advice.

Right Bob Taylor, nicknamed Chat for his quiet and unfussy approach to everything, set a tremendous example in training. We were all delighted that such a popular member of the party was to equal Wasim Bari's Test record of seven victims in an innings during the Bombay Jubilee Test.

Beards and moustaches were very much in vogue on tour, Peter Willey being one of those who found it gave protection from sunburn. Graham Gooch stuck to his military moustache.

David Gower, the most natural stroke-maker in the team, seen during one of his happier innings against the West Indies at Brisbane.

one turned or held and there was a little bit there for all the bowlers.

Wiener was a bit unlucky against me when my arm ball went off his pads and on to the stumps.

McCosker is very much an on-side player and tends to play across the line so that he often directs the ball pitching around the off stump towards the on side. If it holds up you are always likely to have him edging a chance to the wicketkeeper and it happened in this situation, bringing me my 99th wicket against Australia.

Ian Chappell has always persisted in sweeping me to such an extent that we always joke about him bringing out his broom when I'm bowling! This time he got an inside edge that thudded into his pads and flew out on the off side where Ian Botham a yard away made a magnificent catch one-handed, qualifying for the 'Catch of the Season' competition run by Channel Nine television.

So my quicker ball had landed me an historic bowling milestone. I had joined such distinguished names as Wilfred Rhodes, Sydney Barnes, Alec Bedser our manager, and Bobby Peel, the only Englishmen who have taken a century of wickets against Australia.

At 98 for 3 we felt we were still slightly in the hunt, but deep down knew we wanted another breakthrough to make Australia panic.

Kim Hughes came in and dominated from the start. It became a completely different game after lunch, with the wicket playing on the final day as you might expect a normal Test wicket to play on the second day.

Hughes and Greg Chappell hurried Australia to victory by six wickets with more than a day to spare, Australia's captain afterwards proclaiming that as far as they were concerned they had won the Ashes regardless of whether England had refused to put them up for battle.

We had declined to contest the Ashes on the grounds that this was a hastily arranged series, an experimental tour and that the Ashes were normally fought for over a rubber of five Tests and not three. I don't think it mattered to the players on either side, nor do I think it made any difference to the Australian public, except that it gave them the chance to call us whingeing Poms once more.

England versus Australia remains a deadly serious business whether or not the Ashes are available. So our overall disappointment at losing 2–0 was tempered slightly by the knowledge that we had recovered so well after our disastrous first innings score of 123.

We would be going to Melbourne for the Third and final Test with the emphasis very much on our playing for pride and to show that there was not that much of a gap between the two teams.

2nd TEST v. AUSTRALIA

Played at Sydney, 4–9 January 1980. **Australia won by 6 wickets.**

ENGLAND

G. A. Gooch	b Lillee	18	c G. Chappell b Dymock	4
G. Boycott	b Dymock	8	c McCosker b Pascoe	18
D. W. Randall	c G. Chappell b Lillee	0	(6) c Marsh b G. Chappell	25
P. Willey	c Wiener b Dymock	8	(3) b Pascoe	3
*J. M. Brearley	c Pascoe b Dymock	7	(4) c Marsh b Pascoe	19
D. I. Gower	b G. Chappell	3	(7) not out	98
I. T. Botham	c G. Chappell b Pascoe	27	(8) c Wiener b G. Chappell	0
†R. W. Taylor	c Marsh b Lillee	10	(9) b Lillee	8
G. R. Dilley	not out	22	(10) b Dymock	4
R. G. D. Willis	c Wiener b Dymock	3	(11) c G. Chappell b Lillee	1
D. L. Underwood	c Border b Lillee	12	(5) c Border b Dymock	43
Extras	(NB5)	5	(B1, LB10, W1, NB2)	14
Total		123		237

Fall of wickets: 1–10, 2–13, 3–31, 4–38, 5–41, 6–74, 7–75, 8–80, 9–98. 1–6, 2–21, 3–29, 4–79, 5–105, 6–156, 7–174, 8–211, 9–218.

AUSTRALIA

R. B. McCosker	c Gower b Willis	1	(2) c Taylor b Underwood	41
J. M. Wiener	run out	22	(1) b Underwood	13
I. M. Chappell	c Brearley b Gooch	42	c Botham b Underwood	9
*G. S. Chappell	c Taylor b Underwood	3	not out	98
K. J. Hughes	c Taylor b Botham	18	c Dilley b Willis	47
A. R. Border	c Gooch b Botham	15	not out	2
†R. W. Marsh	c Underwood b Gooch	7		
D. K. Lillee	c Brearley b Botham	5		
G. Dymock	c Taylor b Botham	4		
L. S. Pascoe	not out	10		
J. D. Higgs	b Underwood	2		
Extras	(B2 LB12 W2)	16	(LB8 W1)	9
Total		145	(4 wkts)	219

Fall of wickets: 1–18, 2–52, 3–71, 4–92, 5–100, 6–114, 7–121, 8–129, 9–132.   1–31, 2–51, 3–98, 4–203.

BOWLING

AUSTRALIA	*O*	*M*	*R*	*W*	*O*	*M*	*R*	*W*
Lillee	13.3	4	40	4	24.3	3	63	2
Dymock	17	6	42	4	28	8	48	3
Pascoe	9	4	14	1	23	3	76	3
G. Chappell	4	1	19	1	21	10	36	2
Higgs	1	0	3	0				
ENGLAND								
Botham	17	7	29	4	23.3	12	43	0
Willis	11	3	30	1	12	2	26	1
Underwood	13.2	3	39	2	26	6	71	3
Dilley	5	1	13	0	12	0	33	0
Willey	1	0	2	0	4	0	17	0
Gooch	11	4	16	2	8	2	20	0

6. The Third Test

A highlight of the Melbourne Test was Dennis Lillee celebrating his 200th Test match wicket and bowling us into submission. His marathon match analysis of 66.1 overs, 15 maidens, 138 runs and 11 wickets tells only half the story of the best all-round bowling performance England had seen from Lillee since his great-hearted display in the Centenary Test on the same ground in March 1977. He joined four famous Australians who have taken more than 200 wickets in Test cricket, Richie Benaud (248), Graham McKenzie (246), Ray Lindwall (228) and Clarrie Grimmett (216).

But what has been more remarkable about Lillee's achievement is that he reached this great bowling milestone in only 38 Test matches compared with 63 appearances by Benaud, 60 by McKenzie and 61 by Lindwall. Only the legendary Grimmett (37 Tests) took his wickets for Australia in the time that Lillee has in modern Test cricket.

Talking with other England players about Dennis we pondered on the bowling heights he might well have scaled had he not missed some forty Test matches in his ten-year career on account of a crippling back injury in the early 1970s and of course his playing with WSC for two years.

Lillee had every right to be feeling tired after playing in three Tests against the West Indies and two against us. He was suffering from a virus on the first day but bowled quite magnificently taking 2 for 36 in 20 overs in a situation where he would have been entitled to have eased off, Australia having already won the series.

We thought we ought to be able to take advantage of the

Australians, expecting them to be pretty depressed after their massive 408 runs defeat by the West Indies in Adelaide two days earlier, a result which left them flattened 2–0.

Greg Chappell, their captain, had even warned his players on the eve of the final Test that several of them had their international cricket careers at stake. He went as far as declaring publicly, 'Many players' careers could be affected by this game. It's important for them to realize that it's not a matter of playing for the team, but for their cricketing futures. I can jump up and down, but a lot has to come from the individual.' These were strong comments for any Test captain to make and for the first three hours of the first day's play the Australians looked anything but motivated in the field.

I thought several of them appeared jaded as a result of being forced to play two Test matches almost on top of one another, a system they will surely abandon in 1980–81 when they take on India and New Zealand.

Geoff Boycott and Graham Gooch shared in a partnership of 116, by far the best start we had in any innings of the series.

Geoff was all set for another long innings when he was superbly caught low down by Ashley Mallett in the gully. From a captain's point of view gully is a difficult position in which to place your catcher just right, because the ball comes off the face of the bat that much faster than it does when snicked to the slips.

Although we had got off to such a sound start it had not been easy for Wayne Larkins (Ned), who had sat for 148 minutes in the dressing-room waiting to play his maiden Test innings. I suggested to Ian Botham that it would possibly be a good idea for someone to relieve Larkins if a wicket had not fallen by the time mid-afternoon drinks were taken. It can be extremely tiring concentrating on every ball and feeling you could be out there any moment.

Some batsmen don't find it that easy when they have a long wait sitting, watching and concentrating on every ball; it can be very difficult to keep yourself geared up, but the captain decided that the batting order should not be altered. As it happened, a wicket fell prior to the drinks interval and Larkins batted as the ideal foil to Gooch. At one time we were able to sit back and relax looking at the scoreboard that read 170 for 1.

But middle-order disasters overtook us as they had in all four previous innings in this campaign against Australia. For instance, Gooch was entitled to think that his first Test 100 was just around the corner. He had got to 99 and was facing the last over before tea when he stroked Len Pascoe's second delivery straight down the wicket, hesitated and then called David Gower for a single not appreciating that the ball was travelling slowly enough for Kim Hughes to intercept as he ran from mid-off.

Gooch had committed himself and just failed to get home as Hughes's throw broke the wicket. Ironically his wife Brenda had just been interviewed on television as she sat anxiously in the stand waiting for Graham's first Test century. I am not sure who looked more crestfallen, Brenda or Gooch, as he walked off with head bowed in despair.

Afterwards Graham blamed himself for our latest middle order collapse which saw us slip from a 170 for 1 to 192 for 6. Probably if he hadn't been so keyed up about his first century in a Test he would not have taken the risk. 'I didn't want to do anything silly in that last over,' he said. 'I have no one to blame but myself. I went half forward and was only really stopping the ball, not looking for a run. But the ball went off the middle of the bat straighter and faster than I expected, it all happened so quickly. I thought, here we go, and miscalled. It was my fault. The thing that was so awful was that losing my wicket seemed to lead to our collapse.'

It meant that we had two new batsmen, Gower and Botham, both having to play themselves in at the same time after the interval. We thought Botham was a bit unlucky as he did not appear to get a touch when aiming to turn the ball down the leg side. Brearley and Bob Taylor prevented the collapse from becoming a complete crisis and lifted us to 231 for 6 by the close. It had been surprising to see so many overs of spin after poor Jim Higgs had been allowed a solitary over with his leg-breaks at Sydney. Suddenly we saw 33 overs bowled in a day by Mallett and almost half the runs came off him.

What seemed odd was that if Lillee, Dymock and Pascoe were feeling the effects of a hard Test in Adelaide, why on earth didn't Chappell bowl himself and Alan Border instead of relying on just four bowlers that day?

The ball was moving around a fair bit on the second morning and Taylor, myself and John Lever became Lillee's 198th, 199th and 200th Test victims.

Mike Brearley gave some of the recognized batsmen an object lesson in concentration, stubbornly hanging on for nearly four hours for his unbeaten 60. His best allies had been Taylor and Lever who stretched our first innings to the slightly more respectable total of 306.

That man Lillee still finished with 6 for 60 and another extraordinary statistic was revealed about him: the fact that in his last fifteen Tests he had captured 100 wickets at the same time bringing his total against England to 111. In this innings he had slowed his pace down and genuinely used the leg-cutter, pulling down on the side of the ball with the effect of producing deliveries that resembled fast leg-breaks. He had been typically clever when crowding the bat to prise out Lever. With four men crouching round the bat and Lever expecting a lifting delivery he slipped in a marvellous delivery on a full-length which cut back the ball and was played on to the stumps.

I managed to get McCosker again with Botham picking up the catch at short mid-on. It held up a fraction but that was to be our only success as this Test started slipping away from us once more.

Bruce Laird plodded along in his unflappable manner and

with Ian Chappell in such command with Australia on 155 for 1 at the close Sunday promised to be one of those days when we would get the run-around.

It gave me some satisfaction having Ian Chappell caught and bowled especially after I failed to grasp with my right hand one that he drove murderously hard back at me much earlier in his innings.

The first session of play had been one of the better ones for me. Bowling a bit slower I deceived Laird and tempted him to drive. It's not a shot that he plays powerfully and almost turning the delivery into a full toss he presented David Gower with a catch at mid-wicket.

At about that stage I had taken 3 for 49 in 26 overs, an analysis which was to read less favourably later on when I was annoyed with myself for not coming back to bowl the same way.

Throughout the series, and especially on this occasion, I had problems when coming back to bowl later in the day and put some of the difficulties down to bowling so few first-class overs in between the Tests. To be in a rhythm I need to bowl a lot. I had to break when the new ball was taken but I was still finding it hard to make an impact in my second spell.

Greg Chappell, whom I've got out thirteen times in Test cricket, played me better than at any other time in the series. Chappell had plenty of support from his front-line batsmen in grinding us down.

Nobody was a better example of this than Alan Border who used his feet so well, twice hitting me over the top. Their overnight lead of 93 was developed into an overall advantage of 171. Lever got his reward towards the end of their innings, adopting the rôle of the stock bowler after I'd received some punishment.

When we batted again the feeling was that the wicket was playing truer and there was no reason for us not to bat long enough to avoid defeat. We should have been more wary of what Lillee might do again. Not charging in with his usual new-ball ferocity, he reverted to his cutters and bowled an immaculate line; his variations of pace were confusing too and we had the unusual sight of Boycott being bowled as he shouldered arms, an amazing dismissal for him.

Gooch played with the same authority he had shown in the first innings, only to miss a straight one from Mallett after getting his 50. With Gower being bowled, having played a shot which must have given him nightmares, the old familiar middle-order catastrophe was with us again.

Luckily Botham survived the company of Taylor after we'd collapsed to 92 for 6. It gave us comfort to see him playing much straighter. He'd worked hard in the nets and countered Pascoe with one or two drives that were as good as any shots played in this Test. He resisted going for the pull or hook shots with which Botham scores a lot of runs but which have often led to his downfall.

It would need an exceptional innings even by his inspired standards to save us from another defeat. On 157 for 6 at the end of another bad day we were still 14 behind Australia. The result looked a formality.

We agreed that the tactics for the tail would be to give Botham his head and for us to defend grimly at the other end on a wicket where the odd ball tended to keep remarkably low.

In terms of time consumed Lever did even better than the gallant Taylor, staying for 106 minutes whilst Botham kept the score moving at the other end. I hadn't been much help to him in the midst of our belated rearguard action. I was almost bowled first ball by Pascoe, and Botham came down the wicket with some advice: 'Deadly, you must get forward on this track as the odd one's keeping low.' The next one took off, rapping me on the gloves painfully. So much for Botham's guidance!

We met in mid-wicket with Ian thinking it a tremendous joke

and me saying, 'Thanks very much for your advice, mate, a lot of help that was.' I got nowhere near the next one; it sent my off stump flying in the direction of the slips.

I doubt whether any of Botham's six Test centuries have given him as much pleasure as this one, because up to then his batting average was around 8.00 and was a topic one didn't debate too much in his presence.

He gets away with playing so many adventurous shots, partly because of wonderful timing and partly because he hits the ball so hard that it carries over fielders set in normal catching positions. The Australians should have dismissed him on 54 when Dymock put him down at deep square leg. Botham was the first to thank Lever for keeping him company whilst he bulldozed his way to 119 not out. Altogether Lever batted for 197 minutes in the match, and showed how difficult he can be to dig out. His defensive technique is advanced by tail-end standards and I am sure that if he didn't bowl so many overs for Essex he would have developed into a respectable county standard number seven or eight.

The Australians required 103 to make it a clean sweep in the three-match rubber and had all the time they wanted to make the runs. We bowled very professionally at McCosker and Laird, who refused to take any chances. Their caution was replaced by a different approach from their captain, who refused to be bogged down, but we had done well enough to take this Test into the mandatory final 20 overs. In the first of these Greg, applauded by his brother at the other end, took the Australians to victory for the second time in successive Tests.

As we walked off with Mike Brearley congratulating his counterpart I reflected that it was a doubly sad occasion for senior players such as Mike, Geoff Boycott, Bob Willis, Bob Taylor and myself who could not expect to be back on the next tour of Australia scheduled for 1982–3. We had to resign ourselves to this being our farewell Test down under.

As we reached the dressing-room we heard that Australia's fast bowling idol Lillee had quite rightly been voted Man of the Match and Man of the Series. He'd kept coming at us and never allowed us to get back into this Test from the time we had been 170 for 1, a situation which turned out to be too good to be true.

3rd TEST v. AUSTRALIA

Played at Melbourne, 1–6 February 1980. **Australia won by 8 wickets.**

ENGLAND

G. A. Gooch	run out	99	b Mallett	51
G. Boycott	c Mallett b Dymock	44	b Lillee	7
W. Larkins	c G. Chappell b Pascoe	25	lbw b Pascoe	3
D. I. Gower	lbw b Lillee	0	b Lillee	11
P. Willey	lbw b Pascoe	1	c Marsh b Lillee	2
I. T. Botham	c Marsh b Lillee	8	(7) not out	119
*J. M. Brearley	not out	60	(6) c Border b Pascoe	10
†R. W. Taylor	b Lillee	23	c Border b Lillee	32
D. L. Underwood	c I. Chappell b Lillee	3	b Pascoe	0
J. K. Lever	b Lillee	22	c Marsh b Lillee	12
R. G. D. Willis	c G. Chappell b Lillee	4	c G. Chappell b Pascoe	2
Extras	(B1, LB2, NB14)	17	(B2, LB12, NB10)	24
Total		306		273

Fall of wickets: 1–116, 2–170, 3–175, 4–177, 5–177, 6–192, 7–238, 8–242, 9–296, 10–306.

1–25, 2–46, 3–64, 4–67, 5–88, 6–92, 7–178, 8–179, 9–268, 10–273.

AUSTRALIA

R. B. McCosker	c Botham b Underwood	33	lbw b Botham	2
B. M. Laird	c Gower b Underwood	74	c Boycott b Underwood	25
I. M. Chappell	c and b Underwood	75	not out	26
K. J. Hughes	c Underwood b Botham	15		
A. R. Border	c and b Lever	63		
*G. S. Chappell	c Larkins b Lever	114	(4) not out	40
†R. W. Marsh	c Botham b Lever	17		
D. K. Lillee	c Willey b Lever	8		
G. Dymock	b Botham	19		
A. A. Mallett	lbw Botham	25		
L. S. Pascoe	not out	1		
Extras	(B13, LB12, W1, NB7)	33	(LB8, NB2)	10
Total		477	(2 wkts)	103

Fall of wickets: 1–52, 2–179, 3–196, 4–219, 5–345, 6–411, 7–421, 8–432, 9–465, 10–477.

1–20, 2–42.

BOWLING

AUSTRALIA	O	M	R	W	O	M	R	W
Lillee	33.1	9	60	6	33	6	78	5
Dymock	28	6	54	1	11	2	30	0
Mallett	35	9	104	0	14	1	45	1
Pascoe	32	7	71	2	29.5	3	80	4
Border					4	0	16	0
ENGLAND								
Lever	53	15	111	4	7.4	3	18	0
Botham	39.5	15	105	3	12	5	18	1
Willis	21	4	61	0	5	3	8	0
Underwood	53	19	131	3	14	2	49	1
Willey	13	2	36	0				

7. The World Series Cup

From the moment the TCCB accepted Australia's experimental itinerary, albeit with some reduction to the original, we knew we would be committed to a heavy programme of one-day cricket.

Even if we failed to reach the finals of the World Series Cup competition we would be engaged in ten one-day contests as well as three Test matches and only five other games of first-class cricket.

Although the West Indies arrived in Australia with a formidable reputation as the kings of one-day cricket, having twice won the Prudential World Cup in England, we fancied our chances because of the wealth of experience English players have in playing the limited-overs game.

The World Series Cup was clearly drawn out on the lines on which we had played our one-day WSC matches. The tournament was run on the basis of Australia, England, and the West Indies all playing each other four times with the two most successful countries then advancing to the finals, which were to be decided over the best of three matches.

Benson and Hedges, the principal sponsors of cricket in Australia, put up more than $274,000 in prize-money, embracing Australia's Test series against us and the West Indies, and the one-day programme.

Each Test was worth $19,000, with $12,000 going to the winning team, $6,000 to the losing team and $1,000 to the Benson and Hedges Player of the Match.

In the initial World Series Cup contests $3,000 went to the winners, $1,500 to the losers and $500 to the Player of the Match.

There were even more impressive rewards for reaching the finals with $32,000 going to the champions, $16,000 to the runners-up and $2,000 to the outstanding player in the finals.

On top of all this the outstanding player of the year stood to win a Holden Commodore Car worth $10,000.

From our experience of one-day cricket at home, we know how essential it is to have a good opening partnership and not lose wickets to the new ball. In vivid contrast to our performances in the Test matches we nearly always started well.

This was clearly illustrated by our opening partnerships in the qualifying games which read; 79 v. West Indies (Brearley and Randall); 71 v. Australia (Boycott and Randall); 78 v. Australia (Boycott and Randall); 41 v. Australia (Boycott and Gooch); 31 v. Australia (Gooch and Larkins); and 40 v. West Indies (Boycott and Gooch).

To have good starts like this obviously creates a basis for the later batsmen to build on and puts the fielding side under greater pressure later in the innings.

England v. West Indies, Sydney, 28 November 1979

The biggest stir at the beginning of our one-day campaign was the dropping of Boycott. He had been hit on the head by a bouncer playing against Combined Universities in Adelaide and hadn't really struck his best form at that stage, whereas Randall had played impressively as an opener.

Also the selectors did not regard the combination of Boycott and Brearley to open the batting as suitable for the demands of instant cricket. Regarding the pace at which they played an innings they were too similar as openers.

So Randall and Brearley opened in what was going to be a vital first match for us against the West Indies who had overwhelmed England in the Prudential World Cup Final at Lord's in June 1979.

The West Indies had been surprisingly beaten in their first

night match and apparently one of their players was so incensed with his or the team's performance that he broke the dressing-room door!

One of our other bonuses was the sparkling form of Northamptonshire's Peter Willey, who began with scores of 58 not out, 37 and 64. With runs flowing so freely from the recognized batsmen we were able to set up the tempo in the last 20 overs because we nearly always had wickets in hand.

Willey was also very effective with his off-spinners. Unlike the Australians and the West Indians we relied heavily on our spinners, playing Peter, Geoff Miller and myself. We usually bowled our full quota of 10 overs and in that first night match against the West Indies we sent down 28 out of 55.

Our reliance upon slow bowling explained why we were rather opposed to any restrictions on the number of leg-side fielders. This remained a considerable bone of contention between the Australian Cricket Board and ourselves, and the dispute spilled over, with some Australian Test players and Australian cricket crowds not concealing their dislike for what they called 'negative' on-side field placings.

The Australians were calling for a maximum of five men on the on side. They claimed that with no restriction it encouraged 'leg-side and defensive' bowling. They thought our tactics should be discouraged in order to make everyone bowl straighter and more in the direction of the off stump.

In fairness to our management declining to experiment with some limitation of the number of leg-side fielders, we had not in fact ever played with this prescription in domestic cricket, just as we had not had the chance to try out the circles.

It would have been very difficult for the spinners, especially the off-spinners, to have to bowl with a limit of five men on the on side.

We thought that the wickets we played on in a one-day game were of just the right formula. They were brown in colour and did not offer too much bounce or response for the quicker bowlers. I shall always remember the thrilling last-ball victory over the West Indies because of Randall's unbelievable catch that turned the game for us.

Gordon Greenidge, Lawrence Rowe and Alvin Kallicharran had put the Windies well on course as they chased our total of 211. Andy Roberts was playing well and hit me for a huge 6. He went for another massive on-side hit and there was Randall taking off like a goalkeeper, having made a lot of ground at wide mid-on. He must have been three or four feet off the ground, diving to his right and backwards when he clung on to make a staggering catch.

Not surprisingly this effort won him the Catch of the Season award run by Channel Nine Television. From then on the late-order West Indian batsman got into a panic and, with the game reduced to 47 overs a side because of rain, it came down to them requiring 11 with the last pair together when Botham bowled the final over.

Brearley pushed all his fielders right back on to the boundary pickets, including wicketkeeper David Bairstow who was crouching in front of the sightscreen with one glove off in case he had to throw in quickly. Colin Croft was looking for a four.

The crowd booed and hissed at Brearley for his tactics and there was an almighty outcry from the Australian media that this 'wasn't cricket'. We thought they were making a stupid fuss and pointed out in Brearley's defence that if Croft had swung and got a top edge it would easily have gone over the top for four and we would have lost. As it was, Botham made it a dramatic climax by clipping Croft's leg stump.

Beating the world champions was just the boost we wanted so early in the tournament.

ENGLAND v. WEST INDIES

Played at Sydney, 28 November 1979. **England won on faster scoring rate.**

ENGLAND

D. W. Randall	c Parry b Garner	49
*J. M. Brearley	c Greenidge b Parry	25
D. I. Gower	b Croft	44
G. A. Gooch	c and b Parry	2
P. Willey	not out	58
I. T. Botham	b Garner	11
†D. L. Bairstow	c Murray b Garner	0
G. Miller	b Roberts	4
G. R. Dilley	run out	1
D. L. Underwood	did not bat	
R. G. D. Willis		
Extras	(B4, LB13)	17
Total	(8 wkts)	211

Fall of wickets: 1–79, 2–88, 3–91, 4–160, 5–195, 6–195, 7–210, 8–211.

WEST INDIES

C. G. Greenidge	c Willis b Miller	42
D. L. Haynes	b Dilley	4
L. G. Rowe	lbw b Willis	60
A. I. Kallicharran	run out	44
*C. H. Lloyd	c Brearley b Willis	4
†D. L. Murray	c Gower b Underwood	3
D. R. Parry	b Underwood	4
A. M. E. Roberts	c Randall b Underwood	16
J. Garner	not out	8
M. A. Holding	c Gower b Underwood	0
C. Croft	b Botham	3
Extras	(B1, LB7)	8
Total		196

Fall of wickets: 1–19, 2–68, 3–132, 4–143, 5–144, 6–155, 7–177, 8–185, 9–186, 10–196.

BOWLING

WEST INDIES	*O*	*M*	*R*	*W*
Roberts	9	0	37	1
Holding	9	0	47	0
Croft	10	0	34	1
Garner	10	0	31	3
Parry	10	0	35	2
Kallicharran	2	0	10	0
ENGLAND				
Dilley	6	2	21	1
Botham	7	1	26	1
Underwood	10	0	44	4
Miller	10	0	33	1
Willey	8	0	29	0
Willis	6	0	35	2

Player of the match: P. Willey (England)

Australia v. England, Melbourne, 8 December 1979

Graham Dilley had shown up well in that first night match in Sydney. He looked far and away our quickest bowler and had welcome aggression to back his speed and lift, although Mike Brearley perhaps bowled him for one over too many and Greenidge thrashed him for three boundaries in a row so that an analysis of 9 runs from 5 overs suddenly became 6 overs and 21 runs.

Boycott had been in such immaculate form with scores of 101 not out against Tasmania, 110 and 63 not out against South Australia that he had forced himself back into the side. The captain went down the order, a position he occupied for the rest of the tour with some brave and important innings in both the Tests and the World Series Cup games.

Rather to my surprise I was called on to bowl the last over in Sydney and here again in Melbourne, normally the duty of one of the quicker bowlers. Brearley was reluctant to bring Dilley back at that stage because of his inexperience at this level of international cricket. He wanted to protect him from having to bowl at the death when the pressure was on. It's unusual for a spinner to be employed in those circumstances and I've hardly ever done it for Kent or England. I believe it's more difficult for a slower bowler to contain when the slog is on as a batsman has more time to position himself, improvise and hit the ball.

Boycott, Randall and Willey gave us a tremendous start and although we slipped up a bit in the middle we got home by 3 wickets facing a target of 207. Suddenly England were on top of the table, having played two and won two.

With Brearley at number seven, Bairstow at eight and Dilley coming in at number nine we had the depth in batting, and Bairstow supported Brearley to justify his being preferred to Bob Taylor for the one-day matches.

AUSTRALIA v. ENGLAND

Played at Melbourne, 8 December 1979. **England won by 3 wickets.**

AUSTRALIA

J. M. Wiener	b Botham	7
B. M. Laird	lbw b Dilley	7
A. R. Border	c Willey b Dilley	29
*G. S. Chappell	c Gooch b Willey	92
K. J. Hughes	st Bairstow b Gooch	23
K. D. Walters	c Randall b Gooch	12
†R. W. Marsh	c Bairstow b Willey	14
R. J. Bright	c Gooch b Willey	1
D. K. Lillee	not out	13
R. M. Hogg	c Brearley b Underwood	1
J. Thomson	did not bat	
Extras	(B1, LB5, NB2)	8
Total	(9 wkts)	207

Fall of wickets: 1–15, 2–15, 3–73, 4–114, 5–145, 6–184, 7–193, 8–193, 9–207.

ENGLAND

D. W. Randall	lbw b Bright	28
G. Boycott	c Lillee b Hogg	68
P. Willey	c Marsh b Hogg	37
D. I. Gower	c Marsh b Lillee	17
G. A. Gooch	run out	1
I. T. Botham	c Walters b Hogg	10
*J. M. Brearley	c Marsh b Lillee	27
†D. L. Bairstow	not out	15
G. R. Dilley	not out	0
D. L. Underwood	did not bat	
R. G. D. Willis	did not bat	
Extras	(LB3, NB3)	6
Total	(7 wkts)	209

Fall of wickets: 1–71, 2–134, 3–137, 4–138, 5–148, 6–183, 7–203.

BOWLING

ENGLAND	*O*	*M*	*R*	*W*
Dilley	10	1	30	2
Botham	9	2	27	1
Willis	7	0	28	0
Gooch	6	0	32	2
Underwood	10	0	49	1
Willey	8	0	33	3
AUSTRALIA				
Lillee	10	1	36	2
Hogg	10	2	26	3
Thomson	10	1	49	0
Chappell	8	0	40	0
Bright	9	1	40	1
Walters	2	0	12	0

Player of the match: G. S. Chappell (Australia).

Australia v. England, Sydney, 11 December 1979

There was just no holding Boycott now he was back though he could not have made his 105 in more trying circumstances; he had to contend with the fearful din of a speedway meeting coupled with a noisy fireworks display going on in the neighbouring showground! At one stage, with rockets being fired into the night sky and thunder flashes exploding over the Hill, Geoff had to put up with a pall of pink smoke that drifted across the ground.

When he reached his 100 he turned towards our dressing-room raising both arms on high as much as to say, that'll teach you to leave me out of the one-day games.

Although Geoff had taken to wearing a crash-helmet, this was the first time since facing the West Indians in the Prudential World Cup that I had noticed him attaching the perspex visor.

Because the one-day wickets did not have quite so much bounce they suited Geoff's style of play. On slightly slower wickets, and with his defence, he takes a lot of getting out. In this innings it reminded me of the way he played on the 1970–71 tour of Australia under Ray Illingworth. He was actually hitting over the top and went to his century with a classical off drive against Lillee.

Jeff Thomson was nowhere near as menacing a new ball bowler as he had been in 1974–5 as Lillee's partner when England came home shell-shocked. In Melbourne his ten overs cost 49 runs and in Sydney he was even more expensive taking one for 53 in 9.

We were puzzled by some of the comings and goings in Australia's one-day selection. Rodney Hogg was struggling for fitness and we did not see him again, but Maxie Walker bowled most economically in Sydney, only to be abruptly dismissed from Australia's squad.

They had got the blend right in terms of mixing WSC players

with the rebuilt Australian XI by the time of the Second Test, but they did not seem to be able to make up their minds as to whom they wanted for the one-day game.

Trevor Laughlin, like Walker, suffered cruelly. The Victorian all-rounder bowled tightly enough considering we ran up our best one-day total of 264, and then he made a fighting 74 after Australia had collapsed hopelessly to 39 for 5. We just could not understand why we never saw him again.

Such a collapse exposes the drawback to one-day cricket because once a side has got into those kind of straits the game is over as a worthwhile contest, unlike Test cricket where one has a second chance and no limitation of overs in which to build a recovery. The Sydney crowd, or at least those near the members' enclosures and the Bradman Stand were able to enjoy an amusing one-man sideshow as Randall clowned about on the boundary giving a fashion parade with an assortment of hats. He was funniest of all when he pinched a policeman's cap and did his imitation of Charlie Chaplin's walk. England winning by 72 runs were comfortably at the top of the Benson and Hedges table with a maximum six points from three games.

AUSTRALIA v. ENGLAND

Played at Sydney, 11 December 1979. **England won by 72 runs.**

ENGLAND

D. W. Randall	run out	42
G. Boycott	b Lillee	105
P. Willey	c Walker b Chappell	64
D. I. Gower	c Wiener b Lillee	7
G. A. Gooch	b Thomson	11
I. T. Botham	c Walters b Lillee	5
†D. L. Bairstow	c sub b Lillee	18
*J. M. Brearley	not out	2
G. R. Dilley	did not bat	
D. L. Underwood	did not bat	
R. G. D. Willis	did not bat	
Extras	(LB6, W1, NB3)	10
Total	(8 wkts)	264

Fall of wickets: 1–78, 2–196, 3–220, 4–236, 5–242, 6–246, 7–264.

AUSTRALIA

W. M. Darling	c Randall b Willis	20
J. M. Wiener	st Bairstow b Willey	14
A. R. Border	b Willey	1
*G. S. Chappell	run out	0
K. J. Hughes	c Bairstow b Willis	1
K. D. Walters	c Bairstow b Botham	34
†R. W. Marsh	b Dilley	12
T. J. Laughlin	c Gooch b Randall	74
D. K. Lillee	b Botham	14
J. Thomson	run out	0
M. H. N. Walker	not out	9
Extras	(LB10, W2, NB1)	13
Total		192

Fall of wickets: 1–33, 2–36, 3–36, 4–38, 5–39, 6–63, 7–115, 8–146, 9–147, 10–192.

BOWLING

AUSTRALIA	*O*	*M*	*R*	*W*
Lillee	10	0	56	4
Thomson	9	0	53	1
Walker	10	1	30	0
Laughlin	8	0	39	0
Border	4	0	24	0
Chappell	5	0	28	1
Walters	3	0	24	0
ENGLAND				
Dilley	9	0	29	1
Botham	10	1	36	2
Willis	10	1	32	2
Willey	5	0	18	2
Underwood	6	1	29	0
Gooch	7	0	33	0
Randall	0.2	0	2	1

Player of the match: G. Boycott (England).

West Indies v. England, Brisbane, 23 December 1979.

Randall's first-ball dismissal heralded the start of a miserable run for one of the most popular members of the party. But Gower and Willey kept it going while Boycott was strangely out of touch. This was underlined by him pushing 40 singles in a score of 65, and he said afterwards that he just couldn't hit the ball properly.

Our tea-time debate concluded that our 217 was probably 30 or 40 runs short of what we needed on the smallest of Australia's

Test Ovals. We really needed a repeat of our previous score at Sydney. A good start for us was essential when West Indies batted.

The West Indies, after their disastrous run in the Cup, were starting to fire as only they can when their batsmen are in the mood. Greenidge and Desmond Haynes plundered 20 off the first 4 overs from Botham and Dilley. Greenidge appeared to have definite policies in this sort of cricket. If Haynes stayed with him he would try to push the score along early on, but if Haynes went quickly then he regarded as his prime responsibility to help play-in the mighty Viv Richards, and let Viv take over. It said something for the quality of Viv's latest batting extravaganza that he actually caught up Gordon after coming in with the score at 109 for 1.

When two of the greatest batsmen in the world get in on a wicket like that there's not much you can do about it. People say bowl a line and a length but players like Gordon and Viv take a lot of holding and are capable of destroying any bowling.

ENGLAND v. WEST INDIES

Played at Brisbane, 23 December 1979. **West Indies won by 9 wickets.**

ENGLAND

D. W. Randall	c Lloyd b Roberts	0
G. Boycott	c sub b Holding	68
P. Willey	run out	34
D. I. Gower	c Holding b Roberts	59
G. A. Gooch	b Garner	17
I. T. Botham	lbw b Holding	4
†D. L. Bairstow	c Lloyd b Roberts	12
*J. M. Brearley	not out	9
G. R. Dilley	b Garner	0
D. L. Underwood	did not bat	
R. G. D. Willis	did not bat	
Extras	(LB8, W5, NB1)	14
Total	(8 wkts)	217

Fall of wickets: 1–0, 2–70, 3–167, 4–174, 5–191, 6–205, 7–209, 8–217.

WEST INDIES

C. G. Greenidge	not out	85
F. L. Haynes	c Underwood b Gooch	41
I. V. A. Richards	not out	85
A. I. Kallicharran	did not bat	
L. G. Rowe	did not bat	
*C. H. Lloyd	did not bat	
C. L. King	did not bat	
†D. L. Murray	did not bat	
J. Garner	did not bat	
A. M. E. Roberts	did not bat	
M. A. Holding	did not bat	
Extras	(LB4, NB3)	7
Total	(1 wkt)	218

Fall of wickets: 1–109.

BOWLING

WEST INDIES	*O*	*M*	*R*	*W*
Roberts	10	3	26	3
Holding	10	1	44	2
Garner	10	0	37	2
Richards	10	0	44	0
King	10	0	52	0
ENGLAND				
Botham	10	1	39	1
Dilley	8	1	25	0
Willis	10	2	27	0
Underwood	9	0	43	0
Willey	6	0	39	0
Gooch	3.5	0	38	1

Player of the match: C. G. Greenidge (West Indies).

Australia v. England, Sydney, 26 December 1979

I will never forget this game for the outrageous behaviour of Ian Chappell and Dennis Lillee towards our captain at the end of Australia's innings.

I've always believed that however intense the cricket is and whatever the pressure one should always show respect for fellow professionals. It upset me to see both Dennis and Ian mocking Mike Brearley and taunting him in front of a crowd of over twenty-one thousand, quite apart from thousands watching the game on television.

From successive deliveries in the last over of Australia's innings, Brearley had chances to run out Lillee but first missed the stumps with a throw from mid-on and then fumbled a return when he was up at the stumps. Lillee stood back applauding him and pointing to the wicket as if to say, that's where you should have thrown it. Worse followed when he demonstrated how to cup one's hand together for a catch. Ian Chappell had to get in on the act after batting so well, and he arrogantly tried to orchestrate England's field placings, waving his bat as a suggestion that Brearley should put a few more men out into the deep.

The Australians were still agitated by our defensive field placing. I felt let down by both Dennis and Ian whose behaviour could have been misinterpreted as being a by-product of the way WSC players conducted themselves on the field. I remembered one incident which reflected badly on WSC and, needless to say, it involved Chappell. In one of the Super-Tests between the world and Australia we wanted 4 to win with 5 wickets standing, so Chappell picked up the ball and deliberately bowled a wide that was so far outside the leg stump that it went to the boundary. After this stupid act Chappell turned round and marched off the field.

Lillee and Chappell may have thought they were being funny when they ridiculed Brearley and may have seen their gestures as gamesmanship to goad the crowd into a greater anti-Pom and in particular anti-Brearley mood. But their behaviour was not becoming from two of Australia's most talented cricketers. I thought that what they did was totally unwarranted and was amazed that no one from Australian cricketing officialdom bothered to reprimand them either privately or publicly. Maybe Chappell and Lillee were just not aware of how they were insulting the great game of cricket. I thought that what Lillee did in abusing Brearley was far worse than his bat-throwing tantrums at Perth. I wondered how many times Australian players had to bring the game into disrepute before any action was taken against them. Goodness knows what kind of influence this sort of behaviour must have on the youth of Australia. I got the impression that the Australian cricket authorities feared a public outcry if they had shown courage by suspending Chappell for his various outbursts of temper and Lillee for his taunting of our captain.

If an England player had been involved in this sort of incident he would have been severely reprimanded and action would have been taken. I remember John Snow on the spur of the moment obstructing Sunil Gavaskar during a Test at Lord's. He was dropped for the next Test. The England team had the impression that Chappell and Lillee were intent at times on trying to be bigger than the game and it appeared that they enjoyed flaunting authority.

Considering this match was played on Boxing Day it had anything but the spirit of Christmas Goodwill!

Before his unnecessary baiting of Brearley, Ian Chappell played one of the finest innings we had seen in the World Series Cup competition. He'd come in with Australia on 109 for 4 in the 33rd over and played some quite brilliant strokes with the crowd roaring him on. However, his undefeated 60 came out of the modest total of 194 for 6.

Boycott making a handsome 86 and Willey 51 swept us to 152 for 2. We could hardly fail after that kind of start, although Rodney Hogg came back to bowl like the wind, 5 wickets disappearing for 27 runs before the Yorkshire combination of Boycott and Bairstow ensured that Brearley had the last laugh over the men who had goaded him so cruelly earlier on.

AUSTRALIA v. ENGLAND

Played at Sydney, 26 December 1979. **England won by 4 wickets.**

AUSTRALIA

B. M. Laird	b Botham	6
J. M. Wiener	c Bairstow b Botham	2
A. R. Border	c Gower b Gooch	22
*G. S. Chappell	run out	52
K. J. Hughes	b Willis	23
I. M. Chappell	not out	60
†R. W. Marsh	c Bairstow b Dilley	10
D. K. Lillee	not out	2
R. M. Hogg	did not bat	
G. Dymock	did not bat	
L. S. Pascoe	did not bat	
Extras	(B3, LB10, NB4)	17
Total	(6 wkts)	194

Fall of wickets: 1–5, 2–21, 3–50, 4–109, 5–135, 6–179.

ENGLAND

G. A. Gooch	lbw b Hogg	29
G. Boycott	not out	86
P. Willey	b Pascoe	51
D. I. Gower	c Marsh b Hogg	2
D. W. Randall	c G. Chappell b Pascoe	1
I. T. Botham	lbw b Hogg	6
*J. M. Brearley	c Marsh b Hogg	0
†D. L. Bairstow	not out	7
G. R. Dilley	did not bat	
D. L. Underwood	did not bat	
R. G. D. Willis	did not bat	
Extras	(LB1, W1, NB11)	13
Total	(6 wkts)	195

Fall of wickets: 1–41, 2–152, 3–157, 4–170, 5–179, 6–179.

BOWLING

ENGLAND	*O*	*M*	*R*	*W*
Dilley	10	1	32	1
Botham	9	1	33	2
Willis	10	1	38	1
Underwood	10	2	36	0
Gooch	8	0	38	1
AUSTRALIA				
Lillee	10	0	47	0
Pascoe	10	2	28	2
Hogg	10	0	46	4
Dymock	10	1	38	0
G. Chappell	5.1	0	23	0

Player of the match: G. Boycott (England).

West Indies v. England, Melbourne, 12 January 1980

England stormed into the $50,000 final of the Benson and Hedges World Series Cup without a ball being bowled at the Melbourne Cricket Ground. Overnight thunderstorms forced this game to be abandoned after rainwater had found its way under the covers. It meant that England had nine points from six matches and these were enough to guarantee our place in the finals.

At that stage, with everyone having played six games, West Indies had five points to Australia's four. Australia would have to win both of their remaining games against England and the West Indies and would be relying on England to beat the West Indies in Adelaide to snatch a place in the finals.

Australia v. England, Sydney, 14 January 1980

I had lost my place in the one-day team. The thinking behind my being left out was that I had played a lot in WSC against the Windies and that maybe they were used to playing me in the limited-overs game, whereas they didn't know quite so much about John Emburey's off-breaks. John is a very efficient one-day bowler and his batting is a plus compared with mine. I had been going for 3.5 to 4 runs an over and quite understood my being dropped; I would have been much more disappointed had I been discarded from the Test side.

Because we had qualified for the finals it gave us a wonderful opportunity of bringing in men who had not experienced night cricket before, such as Wayne Larkins, John Lever and Graham Stevenson. In blistering heat with the temperature soaring to over 100°F, Stevenson destroyed the Australians who tumbled from 148 for 3 to 163 all out. We needed the modest 55 overs total of 164 but had our own problems with Lillee, urged on by the Hill, getting us into an awful mess. No bowler produced such remarkable analyses during the tournament as Dennis's

10–6–12–4 that night. Boycott was injured but Gooch held us together after we had reached 61 for 6.

He made 69 out of 105 for 7 and some level-headed batting by Emburey, Bairstow and Stevenson saw us home by 2 wickets with 7 balls remaining. When I went out in the drinks buggy the score was 61 for 6, and the ever-optimistic Bairstow greeted me with: 'See you at 164, Deadly!'

A fault in the system by which designated members of the Australian and English cricket media name the Man of the Match was exposed in this game. Their nominations apparently had to be in half an hour before the end of each game to assist the awards ceremony conducted for live television. Lillee got the vote in this match when the players of both teams reckoned that Graham Stevenson deserved the distinction for taking 4 for 33, for running out Dymock with a piece of quick thinking and for his match-winning unbeaten 28 made in a crisis. It was a marvellous performance by Stevo, who had been so worried about his first major appearance for an England team that he had been up half the night being sick from anxiety.

AUSTRALIA v. ENGLAND

Played at Sydney, 14 January 1980. **England won by 2 wickets.**

AUSTRALIA

J. M. Wiener	st Bairstow b Emburey	33
R. B. McCosker	c Brearley b Willey	41
I. M. Chappell	c Randell b Emburey	8
*G. S. Chappell	c Randell b Stevenson	34
K. J. Hughes	c Larkins b Lever	34
A. R. Border	c Bairstow b Lever	0
†R. W. Marsh	c Bairstow b Stevenson	0
D. K. Lillee	lbw b Stevenson	0
G. Dymock	run out	0
J. Thomson	not out	3
L. S. Pascoe	b Stevenson	5
Extras	(LB1, W3, NB1)	5
Total	(48.4 overs)	163

Fall of wickets: 1–74, 2–82, 3–89, 4–148, 5–149, 6–150, 7–150, 8–152, 9–155.

ENGLAND

G. A. Gooch	c McCosker b Pascoe	09
W. Larkins	c Thomson b Lillee	5
P. Willey	lbw b Lillee	0
D. I. Gower	c Marsh b Lillee	3
*J. M. Brearley	b G. Chappell	5
D. W. Randall	c Pascoe b Chappell	0
I. T. Botham	b Lillee	0
†D. L. Bairstow	not out	21
J. E. Emburey	c G. Chappell b Dymock	18
G. B. Stevenson	not out	28
J. K. Lever	did not bat	
Extras	(LB5, W1, NB9)	15
Total	(8 wkts and 48.5 overs)	164

Fall of wickets: 1–31, 2–31, 3–40, 4–51, 5–56, 6–61, 7–105, 8–129.

BOWLING

ENGLAND	*O*	*M*	*R*	*W*
Lever	9	1	11	2
Botham	7	0	33	0
Gooch	3	0	13	0
Stevenson	9.4	0	33	4
Emburey	10	1	33	2
Willey	10	0	35	1
AUSTRALIA				
Thomson	9.5	0	46	0
Dymock	9	1	30	1
Lillee	10	6	12	4
Pascoe	10	0	38	1
G. Chappell	10	3	23	2

Player of the match: D. K. Lillee (Australia).

West Indies v. England, Adelaide, 16 January 1980

If the West Indies had lost to both ourselves and the Australians in their final qualifying games, Australia would have reached the finals against England. So it was easy to understand why for once in this hectic Australian cricket season, the Australian fans were praying for an English victory at the Adelaide Oval. For this reason, and because Adelaide has been practically starved of international cricket we had an attendance close on twenty-five thousand for this game.

Brearley was criticized for not batting on winning the toss. In his defence our best chance of shooting a few of the West Indians out was to exploit any early dampness there might have been in the wicket. Also, the West Indies' policy in WSC had been to put the opposition in. They preferred batting second. This game illustrated our belief that it still pays to include one or two slower bowlers in one-day cricket. John Emburey and Peter Willey were much more economical than John Lever, Graham Stevenson and Graham Gooch.

Inevitably, Viv Richards played another superb innings, this time plundering 88 which followed other scores in the Cup of 153, 62, and 85 not out.

I thought that Kallicharran displayed a welcome touch of sportsmanship when he applauded Botham's staggering caught-and-bowled off the little West Indian. Botham had managed to knock the ball up one-handed and then dived backwards full length to grab the ball, still one-handed, at the second attempt, finishing up prostrate on the wicket not quite believing he had actually taken the catch! In Channel Nine's Catch of the Season competition, this catch came second to Randall's wonder-catch which got rid of Roberts off my bowling in Sydney.

This match really belonged to the Antiguan connection of Richards and Andy Roberts, because Andy blasted our batting aside with some beautifully controlled fast bowling. Nobody could get after him as we collapsed towards a 107-run defeat. Botham thrilled the crowd when he took on his Somerset teammate Viv Richards, hitting successive deliveries for 6 and 4 before he was the victim of another amazing catch, the result of sheer athleticism when Desmond Haynes dived low at midwicket. Botham had come in when we were 68 for 5 chasing 247 and not even one of his special innings could have done the trick at that stage.

ENGLAND v. WEST INDIES

Played at Adelaide, 16 January 1980. **West Indies won by 107 runs.**

WEST INDIES

C. G. Greenidge	c Emburey b Willey	50
D. L. Haynes	c Gooch b Stevenson	26
I. V. A. Richards	b Botham	88
A. I. Kallicharran	c and b Botham	57
C. L. King	run out	12
J. Garner	not out	7
A. M. E. Roberts	not out	0
L. G. Rowe	did not bat	
*C. H. Lloyd		
†D. L. Murray		
M. A. Holding		
Extras	(B1, LB4, NB1)	6
Total	(5 wkts)	246

Fall of wickets: 1–58, 2–115, 3–224, 4–227, 5–245.

ENGLAND

G. A. Gooch	b King	20
*J. M. Brearley	c Murray b Roberts	0
P. Willey	c Lloyd b King	5
W. Larkins	c Lloyd b King	24
D. I. Gower	c sub b King	12
D. W. Randall	b Roberts	16
I. T. Botham	c Haynes b Roberts	22
†D. L. Bairstow	not out	23
G. B. Stevenson	b Roberts	1
J. E. Emburey	c Murray b Roberts	1
J. K. Lever	b Garner	11
Extras	(LB2, W1, NB1)	4
Total		139

Fall of wickets: 1–5, 2–24, 3–31, 4–52, 5–68, 6–98, 7–100, 8–105, 9–109, 10–139.

BOWLING

ENGLAND	*O*	*M*	*R*	*W*
Lever	10	1	54	0
Botham	10	0	35	2
Gooch	2	0	22	0
Stevenson	8	1	53	1
Emburey	10	0	39	0
Willey	10	1	37	1
WEST INDIES				
Roberts	10	5	22	5
Holding	7	0	16	0
King	9	3	23	4
Garner	7.5	3	9	1
Richards	7	0	46	0
Kallicharran	2	0	19	0

Player of the match: A. M. E. Roberts (West Indies).

Derek Randall and myself failing to win the Christmas Day fancy dress competition, although someone thought I was a pretty 'Deadly sheikh'!

We got a vital breakthrough in Australia's second innings at Sydney when I bowled out Julien Wiener. We needed quick wickets to have any chance of winning, with Australia being 25–0 chasing 216 at the start of the fourth day.

Ian Botham expresses special delight after clutching a remarkable one-handed catch against his old adversary Ian Chappell. Further celebrations followed as the lads congratulated me on my 100th wicket in Tests against Australia.

Big Bob Willis pondering on the best way of hanging on while David Gower moved up through the 90s at Sydney. Unfortunately the combination of slipfielder Greg Chappell and bowler Lillee was to prise him out a few moments later, leaving Lulu high and dry on 98!

Nightwatchman Underwood literally edging his way towards his highest Test score of 45 made back in 1968 against Australia. By staying for the whole of the morning session, or rather surviving, I won a crate of beer from Ian Botham.

Derek Randall congratulates me on coming through those two torrid hours as nightwatchman. Ian Botham was waiting at the dressing-room door with a lit cigarette saying: 'Deadly, I reckon you need this!'

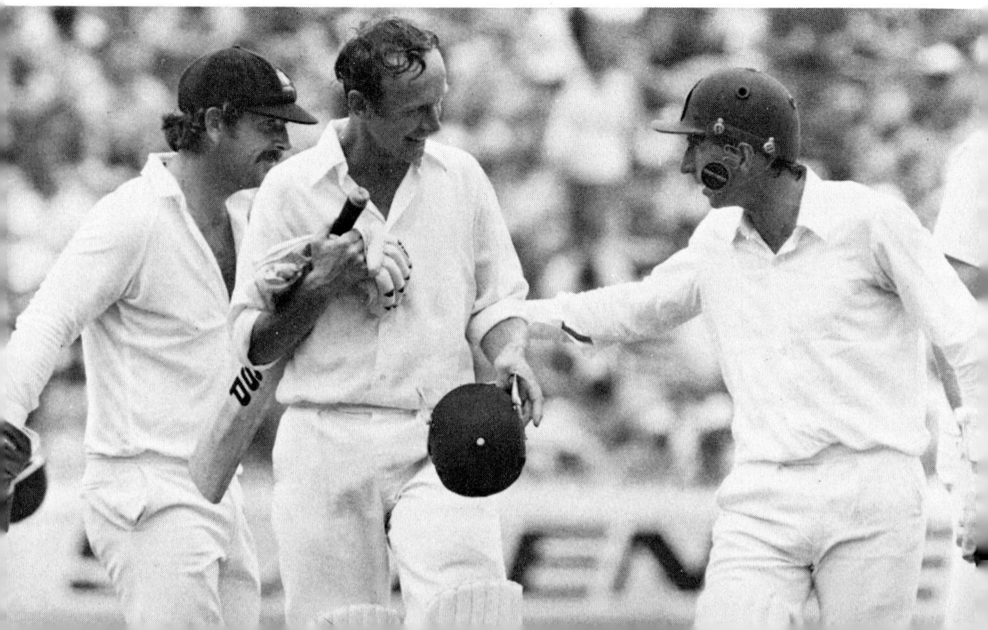

One of the six mighty pylons that now tower over Sydney Cricket Ground lighting everything up so well that England players admitted the light was better than they often encountered on grey, gloomy days back at home.

David Bairstow and Graham Gooch battling away against the mighty Lillee in their royal blue pads, an absolute necessity when using a white ball at night.

A Melbourne streaker about to be 'caught behind' by Greg Chappell during Australia's one-day international against the West Indies.

Viv Richards, unquestionably the player of the season, letting Alan Border and Rodney Marsh check that all his teeth are in place after playing one of the very few false shots between the brilliant ones that destroyed both Australia's and our own attacks.

Gordon Greenidge, who batted so well at times that he bore comparison with the West Indies batting maestro Viv, finds himself doing a handstand after missing a slip chance in the Second Test against Australia at Melbourne.

Signing autographs at Canterbury after hearing that I had been recalled for the tour following two years' absence from Test cricket because of my joining WSC.

FINALS

West Indies v. England, Melbourne, 20 January 1980

There really didn't deserve to be a loser in the first of the one-day finals. This was probably the best of all the matches played during the tournament.

When we came to being highly self-critical we could blame three dropped catches: when Ian Botham put down Gordon Greenidge when 6, Geoff Boycott shelling one from Kalli on 25, and David Gower missing Collis King on 5. Those three lapses were to prove costly because Greenidge got 80, Kalli 42 and King 31 not out.

After putting the West Indians in to bat we still thought we had done pretty well restricting them to 215 for 8. We had been a bit loose towards the end and Bob Willis's last 4 overs cost 39. He had bowled so well earlier with the new ball, but at that stage could not rediscover the same length and line.

If we talked about our catching lapses proving so crucial, so too were the run-outs that brought the downfall of the Northants pair Peter Willey and Ned Larkins. They had been going so well and had carried us to 152 for 3 when the first run-out disaster occurred.

For someone who had played so little on the tour, Ned had been timing his shots superbly, until he faced a freakish incident. Joel Garner deflected Ned's off-drive into the stumps at the non-striker's end in an unsuccessful attempt to run-out Botham.

The ball broke the stump and ran out to Haynes at mid-on, who had noticed that Ned was coming down the wicket looking for a run. He took a shy at the wicket and his throw beat Ned's desperate attempt to get back to the crease.

After the Northampton pair had gone, we felt victory was just beyond us. Lloyd craftily set the field back in a defensive arrangement when we needed a few boundaries.

Botham threatened to get going, but on only 19 he was the victim of an instinctive catch by Lloyd at mid-wicket which the West Indies captain made look ridiculously easy. On another day that shot could have been worth 4 runs. It left Brearley and Bairstow to try and win the game for us.

A crowd of over thirty-thousand were held spellbound by the action as Brearley and Bairstow scampered ones and twos. They came to the last over, bowled by Holding, wanting 14 and it was asking a lot on this big ground to score such a number against a bowler of his speed and accuracy. Both Brearley and Bairstow had grown accustomed to these situations in the Cup. It boiled down to their needing three runs to tie the game and the captain squeezed the ball in the direction of mid-wicket. With Lloyd prowling not far away, it would need a miracle for them to pinch two let alone three runs. Bairstow ambitiously dashed for a second run but Lloyd had all the time in the world to gently return the ball to the bowler for a run-out. We had come very close, losing by just two runs.

FIRST FINAL: ENGLAND v. WEST INDIES

Played at Melbourne, 20 January 1980. **West Indies won by 2 runs.**

WEST INDIES

C. G. Greenidge	c Larkins b Botham	80
D. L. Haynes	c Bairstow b Willis	9
I. V. A. Richards	c Bairstow b Dilley	23
A. I. Kallicharran	b Botham	42
*C. H. Lloyd	b Botham	4
C. L. King	not out	31
†D. L. Murray	c Bairstow b Dilley	4
A. M. E. Roberts	run out	1
J. Garner	run out	3
M. A. Holding	not out	5
C. Croft	did not bat	
Extras	(LB11, W1, NB1)	13
Total	(8 wkts)	215

Fall of wickets: 1–17, 2–66, 3–161, 4–168, 5–168, 6–181, 7–183, 8–197.

ENGLAND

G. A. Gooch	c King b Holding	9
G. Boycott	c Greenidge b Roberts	35
P. Willey	run out	51
D. I. Gower	c Holding b Roberts	10
W. Larkins	run out	34
I. T. Botham	c Lloyd b Roberts	19
*J. M. Brearley	not out	25
†D. L. Bairstow	run out	4
J. E. Emburey	did not bat	
G. R Dilley	did not bat	
R. G. D. Willis	did not bat	
Extras	(B12, LB12, W1, NB1)	26
Total	(7 wkts)	213

Fall of wickets: 1–13, 2–74, 3–96, 4–152, 5–164, 6–190, 7–213.

BOWLING

ENGLAND	*O*	*M*	*R*	*W*
Willis	10	1	51	1
Botham	10	2	33	2
Emburey	10	0	31	0
Dilley	10	0	39	2
Willey	10	0	48	0
WEST INDIES				
Roberts	10	1	30	3
Holding	10	1	43	1
Garner	10	1	27	0
Croft	10	1	23	0
King	4	0	30	0
Richards	6	1	34	0

West Indies v. England, Sydney, 22 January 1980

There were no arguments as to which side deserved the Cup and the $32,000 first prize two days later when the West Indies beat us overwhelmingly by 8 wickets. Sydney was supposed to be their unlucky ground; they had lost their four previous one-day internationals there.

Our splendid catching and throwing had been a match-winning feature in the qualifying games, but if we were to be honest with ourselves these aspects let us down in both the one-day finals.

Greenidge, for instance, was dropped at 31, 51, and 73 on his way to his unbeaten 98. England were as comprehensively beaten as they had been at Lord's in June 1979 when the West Indies had won the Prudential World Cup.

Brearley had adopted his favourite policy of batting when winning the toss in the night matches at Sydney and from the way he and Gooch began it looked as though we would achieve a score of 230 or 240, so desperately needed against a side like the West Indies, whose array of batting skills can make nonsense of almost any target they are set. Boycott ignored another bout of unfortunate publicity in which he had criticized the captain, and batted as though he had nothing on his conscience.

At Melbourne we had scrambled 64 runs from the 10 overs bowled by King and Richards and this time we managed 57, but Roberts, Holding, and Croft were as mean as ever, showing how they had learned to master the delivery that comes into the batsman's body from short of a length.

Greenidge and Haynes gave the Windies the perfect start with a partnership of 61 and their second success in the best of the three finals became a formality once their master batsman, Richards, had got into his stride with Greenidge. Again the Australian crowd was regally entertained by some strokes that only those two batsmen can play. As two of the central figures in the West Indies' overall triumph in the World Series Cup it seemed appropriate they should be together when the winning run was scored with 15 deliveries to spare.

We had observed how the West Indies got away with a number of balls bowled deliberately down the leg side which should have been called as wides by the umpires. Our bowlers aimed at containing Viv, trying to keep the ball somewhere close to his off stump. He still made room to pick up the gaps and more than justified his title of Player of the Season. Greenidge was named Man of the Finals for his innings of 80 in Melbourne and 98 in Sydney. He must be the envy of opening batsmen the world over, combining such a good defence with attacking shots that are hit with frightening power.

With the West Indians winning the finals 2–0 the third play-off was not needed, giving both teams a welcome couple of days off. We were able to sit back and discuss the strengths of the three countries in the World Series Cup, concluding that the West Indies had become very much more professional. Their trainer, in conjunction with Clive Lloyd, had kept them exceptionally fit and they had obviously given far more thought than usual to working out the best ways of restraining the danger men. They bowled straighter at Peter Willey as the Cup progressed and set special field placings for someone like Gower, stationing a fine leg and a deep square leg or someone back on the fence luring him into giving catches. With their battery of fast bowlers and any number of quick-scoring batsmen they had the best blend for this type of cricket.

By winning the Benson and Hedges World Series Cup and by beating Australia 2–0 in their Test series the West Indies really scooped the pool in terms of sponsorship prize-money. With Viv Richards winning a car after being named Player of the Year, the West Indies received a total of $103,000. In the World Series Cup they collected $50,000 from nine games, including $32,000 for winning the finals against England and $4,000 from Player of the Match awards.

The prize-money table for the Test matches and World Series Cup games reads as follows:

Australia	$57,000
England	$56,000
West Indies	$103,000

SECOND FINAL: ENGLAND v. WEST INDIES

Played at Sydney, 22 January 1980. **West Indies won by 8 wickets.**

ENGLAND

G. A. Gooch	lbw b Garner	23
G. Boycott	c Greenidge b Roberts	63
P. Willey	b Garner	3
D. I. Gower	c Murray b Holding	27
W. Larkins	b Croft	14
I. T. Botham	c King b Roberts	37
†D. L. Bairstow	not out	18
*J. M. Brearley	run out	4
J. E. Emburey	run out	6
G. R. Dilley	did not bat	
R. G. D. Willis	did not bat	
Extras	(B1, LB11, NB1)	13
Total	(8 wkts)	208

Fall of wickets: 1–40, 2–54, 3–118, 4–126, 5–155, 6–188, 7–194, 8–208.

WEST INDIES

C. G. Greenidge	not out	98
D. L. Haynes	b Botham	17
I. V. A. Richards	c Botham b Willey	65
A. I. Kallicharran	not out	8
*C. H. Lloyd	did not bat	
C. L. King	did not bat	
†D. L. Murray	did not bat	
M. A. Holding	did not bat	
A. M. E. Roberts	did not bat	
J. Garner	did not bat	
C. Croft	did not bat	
Extras	(B5, LB10, W5, NB1)	21
Total	(2 wkts)	209

Fall of wickets: 1–16, 2–180.

BOWLING

WEST INDIES	*O*	*M*	*R*	*W*
Roberts	10	3	31	2
Holding	10	1	34	1
Croft	10	3	29	1
Garner	10	0	44	2
Richards	3	0	19	0
King	7	1	38	0
ENGLAND				
Willis	10	0	35	0
Dilley	7	0	37	0
Botham	10	1	28	1
Emburey	9·3	0	48	0
Willey	10	2	35	1
Gooch	1	0	5	0

Player of the finals (based on both matches): C. G. Greenidge (West Indies).

Abbreviated details of qualifying games played between Australia and the West Indies in the World Series Cup.

Played at Sydney, 27 November 1979. **Australia won by 5 wickets.**

West Indies 193 (49.3 overs) (A.I. Kallicharran 49, D.L. Haynes 29, C.L. King 29, D.L. Murray 27; L.S. Pascoe 4–29, A.R. Border 3–36, D.K. Lillee 2–10.)

Australia 196–5 (47.1 overs) (G.S. Chappell 74 n.o., K.J. Hughes 52, B.M. Laird 20; C. Croft 2–30, I.V.A. Richards 2–47.)

Player of the match: G.S. Chappell (Australia).

Played at Melbourne, 9 December 1979. **West Indies won by 80 runs.**

West Indies 271–2 (48 overs) (I. V. A. Richards 153 n.o., D.L. Haynes 80.)

Australia 191–8 (48 overs) (A.R. Border 44, G.S. Chappell 31, J.M. Wiener 27; M.A. Holding 2–29, A.M.E. Roberts 2–33, C.L. King 2–40.)

Player of the match: I.V..A. Richards (West Indies).

Played at Sydney, 21 December 1979. **Australia won by 7 runs.**

Australia 176–6 (50 overs) (I.M. Chappell 63 n.o., R.W. Marsh 33, G.S. Chappell 24.)

West Indies 169 (42.5 overs) (I.V.A. Richards 62, C.G. Greenidge 33; D.K. Lillee 4–28, G.S. Chappell 2–14, G. Dymock 2–28, L.S. Pascoe 2–38.)

Player of the match: I.M. Chappell (Australia).

Played at Sydney, 18 January 1980. **Australia won by 9 runs.**

Australia 190 (48.3 overs) (R.B. McCosker 95, J.M. Wiener 50; M.A. Holding 4–17, D.R. Parry 3–61, A.M.E. Roberts 2–38.)

West Indies 181 (49.1 overs) (A.I. Kallicharran 66, D.L. Murray 35, C.H. Lloyd 34 n.o.; D.K. Lillee 3–17, L.S. Pascoe 3–34, G.S. Chappell 2–37.)

Player of the match: R.B. McCosker (Australia).

8. The Jubilee Test at Bombay

When the Indians come to celebrate a centenary of Test cricket with England, they will recall the Golden Jubilee match which belonged to Ian Botham.

Even by Botham's remarkable standards, his all-round contribution towards our victory was quite staggering. He dominated the match from start to finish, first with his bowling and then with his batting. He took 13 wickets in this celebration Test, and as if his bowling wasn't enough to win us the game almost single-handed – he produced a superb innings of 114 in the wake of yet another England batting crisis.

He arrived in India already hailed as one of England's most exceptional cricketers, following the stories the Indians had taken back from the previous summer's Tests in England. The Indians expected something special from him – and the man they nicknamed 'Mr Iron Bottom' never let them down. The headlines of the Indian papers proclaimed that this Test was a contest between 'India and Mr Iron Bottom' because of the way he dominated each day's play.

They loved his massive hitting when he and Gooch carried off the Murphy double wicket competition, watched by over fifty thousand people, three days before the jubilee celebrations really got under way.

The atmosphere was completely different from Australia, with the Indians according us magnificent hospitality and expressing a sincere delight that we had stopped off in their country to commemorate the 50th Anniversary of the Indian Board of Control.

Some of the team went up to Agra on a sightseeing trip of the

Taj Mahal, which truly deserves its standing as one of the seven wonders of the world. The rest of us took advantage of the splendid shopping facilities in Bombay where silk, leather, jewels and trinkets can be bought in the bustling marketplaces at ridiculously cheap prices.

We found it hard in this relaxed atmosphere to concentrate on the normal build-up for a Test match – nor did we have too many fit men when the Test team was announced for the Jubilee match.

Peter Willey had a pulled thigh muscle, Graham Dilley had a rib strain and Derek Randall had damaged a shoulder when colliding with the boundary fence during the double-wicket competition. Bob Willis was feeling sorry for himself because he had a stomach upset.

With Bob laid up in his hotel bed the management brought me into their selection discussion and on the morning of the match I was asked my views about the final eleven. Initially, I must admit I was taken aback about being part of the selection thinking because I've never liked the feeling that I might be deciding the future career of a fellow professional.

Our biggest debate surrounded whether it was right to play Stevenson as the extra seamer or Bairstow as a batsman who could bolster up our fragile middle-order batting.

Bairstow had done a tremendous job making runs when we needed them so badly in the World Series Cup in Australia, but we were worried about the wicket at the Wankhede Stadium, which had an unusual amount of grass on it. Traditionally the wicket at Bombay encourages the spinners towards the end of a five-day Test and there was still a case for playing Bairstow because he is a good batsman against slow bowling.

In the end everyone was relieved that we included Stevo to back up Botham and Lever.

It seemed odd going into a Test against India and not finding any of their distinguished spinning quartet of the 1970s in their ranks. For most of us it was the first time we had played India without facing at least one of the combination of Bedi, Chandra, Prasanna or Venkat.

There was still the suspicion that the wicket would turn, as the Australians had discovered earlier in the season, and that is why we were anxious to bat first if we won the toss.

The Indians made the most of celebrating their jubilee with a pre-Test parade of their former Test captains and famous characters, including such illustrious names as Mushtaq Ali, Hazare, Pataudi, Umrigar, and men who have left them more recently like Venkat, Contractor and Bedi. The night sky over Bombay had been lit up on the eve of the Test when they staged a spectacular firework display at the Brabourne stadium, once the centre of Test cricket in Bombay.

Whilst the rockets and flares zoomed into the night we were enjoying ourselves nicely at our traditional eve-of-Test get-together in the resplendent Taj Mahal hotel. To make us feel at home the hotel management organized the soothing background music of Beethoven's Fifth Symphony – greatly appreciated by our captain who has been known to hum the opening bars.

The next morning the Indian crowd had plenty of opportunity to practise their singing because of the kind of mix-up that can only happen in a Test match in India. As large coloured balloons floated into the sky they found they were obliged to sing the Indian and British anthems not once – but twice! Nobody seemed to mind and Billy Griffith, the M C C President, stood alongside the British High Commissioner and President of the Indian Cricket Board on a specially constructed dais patiently waiting for the anthems to end and the cricket to start.

It did not take long for us to realize that the wicket was going to be a haven for the seam and swing bowlers. Presumably the groundsmen had left the extra grass on fearing that it might turn early, and the last thing the Indians wanted was for their jubilee celebrations to be terminated quickly.

In fact the spinners hardly bowled and between them took just one wicket in the Test, and that was when Dilip Doshi got John Lever out. I bowled three tiny spells, totalling 7 overs when normally I would have expected to have bowled many more overs.

With Botham, Lever and Stevenson having such success poor John Emburey never got on at all. Sunil Gavaskar made us regret the loss of the toss with the way he assaulted the new ball. He seemed to think it was a carnival and once smote Lever into the top tier of the stand for a glorious six. He went on playing the most extravagant shots with India rushing to 50 in barely half an hour. We could hardly believe we were involved in the opening stages of a Test match.

Gavaskar had great difficulty in buckling down and concentrating and continued to play some hair-raising shots against the new ball. The way the Indians started we thought they would run up a score of 400 before the end of the day, but the mood and scoring rate altered dramatically when Ned Larkins ran Roger Binny out as a result of a quick piece of thinking. We thought Gavaskar was a bit to blame because he called Binny who had pushed away a ball from Stevenson. Ned moved very quickly in the field to pick up the ball, and his direct throw to the bowler's end hit the stumps almost before Gavaskar and Binny had crossed.

All afternoon it looked a different game with Botham and Lever putting us back into contact with the score.

Lever bowled beautifully but with terrible luck. He had numerous lbw decisions turned down and once more we suffered the reaction of overseas umpires who universally seem to refuse to give a batsman out against left-arm fast bowlers delivering over the wicket. Maybe umpires in India are simply not used to this type of bowling, although it struck us they were better disposed towards Ghavri, India's counterpart to Lever.

We reckon that Lever would have finished with four or five wickets had English umpires been standing in this Test. In both innings we could not undervalue his support rôle for Botham because he kept so much pressure on the Indian batsmen at the other end.

Botham had the Indians in so much trouble in mid afternoon that we were thinking in terms of bowling them out for about 200, but we should never have underestimated Syed Kirmani, their wicketkeeper, who has held up some of the best Test attacks in the world in similar circumstances. If Both was our hero on the first day, then Kirmani deserved any medals that were being awarded to the opposition. He got after me at the end of the day and, finishing with an unbeaten 40, lifted India to the more respectable total of 242.

We just could not believe how the Indians managed to leave Kirmani at home when they visited England in 1979. He is an accomplished late-order batsman and a wicketkeeper who would get into most Test teams. He had time and again proved his ability to get useful runs and his prowess in taking the top Indian spin bowlers.

It had been some day, finishing with us congratulating Bob Taylor on equalling the Test wicketkeeping record of seven victims in an innings. Bob and Pakistan's Wasim Bari are the only wicketkeepers to have achieved this feat in Test cricket.

One of the topics of conversation in the dressing-room at the close of play centred on how much the ball swung around for Botham, Lever and Stevenson, and we wondered if it had anything to do with our using Gray Nicolls balls, manufactured in England. Unlike the balls we had come across in Australia, they retained the shine far longer.

Hardly had the Test begun than we found ourselves spending what should have been the second day's play waiting for India's first total eclipse of the sun since 1898. The rest day was brought forward for fear that the players and spectators would damage their eyes by looking up at the sun as the moon obscured it.

Hundreds of Indians queued for hours in downtown bazaars where they bought 'solar goggles' for one rupee in order to witness the eclipse. Bernard Thomas had warned the team that it would be highly dangerous to look at the sun at any stage of the eclipse even through goggles, camera film or sunglasses. We still couldn't miss seeing the effect that the eclipse had on the light in mid afternoon. It lasted for just over seventeen minutes and cast shadows over the hotel. Only a handful of Indians ventured out into the normally busy streets of Bombay, and the city seemed to have come to a standstill.

India's fast bowlers, Kapil Dev and Ghavri, threatened a very different kind of eclipse when our batting ran into its customary problems on tour. With the help of some arguable lbw decisions our first innings subsided to 58 for 5. We felt particularly aggrieved for Brearley who was given out lbw against Dev when leaving a ball that bounced considerably and must have come back a long way.

The umpires and Hanumantha Rao in particular stayed very much in the centre of the action. Bob Taylor had made 7 when Rao instantly gave him out caught behind off Kapil Dev. Dev had appealed but few people around the bat had joined him in claiming the catch. Taylor stood there amazed at first and then started to walk off, looking back after going about fifteen yards. Then he turned and saw the Indian captain Viswanath and the umpire deep in conversation. 'Vishy' had persuaded the umpire to alter his decision because he did not believe that Bob had got a nick on the ball. He led Bob back, apologizing for what had happened, and we could only admire his sporting gesture, something that isn't often seen in Test cricket.

Ironically, Vishy's gentlemanly act worked cruelly against India because instead of being 85 for 6, England were to become

229 for 6 through the inspiration of Botham and the dedication of Taylor at the other end. Botham's 100 was probably an even better innings than the one he played in a similar situation in a previous Test at Melbourne. He improvised a good deal, swept arrogantly and played some devastating square cuts against the quicker bowlers. Once again he got away with one or two risky shots because of the sheer power with which he follows through. Taylor was the perfect compliment to Botham, grafting away and not doing anything irresponsible. He is cast perfectly in the rôle for batting in India, where it's such a game of patience. Our only regret was that Botham was not there to carry on the next day when we were going to need a respectable lead.

Botham's sixth Test century and second in a row against India came in a partnership of 171, surpassing the previous best of 165 by David Gower and Geoff Miller at Edgbaston a year earlier.

Botham, with whom I was sharing a hotel bedroom, made the point that evening that he would follow the example of the Indian batsmen by walking instantly if he got the faintest nick. He was referring to the sporting manner in which certain Indian batsmen had accepted their caught-behind dismissals in the first innings. He was also full of admiration for Vishy's refreshing attitude in bringing Taylor back to the crease after he had been given out. By now the phone in our room never stopped ringing with Indian cricket-lovers wishing to pay their respects to 'Mr Iron Bottom'. Botham graciously accepted their plaudits and patiently posed for one fanatic who had brought half his family to be photographed in the company of England's man of the moment. Another Indian fan had travelled over forty miles by public transport just to come and garland Botham.

The awe with which the Indians came to regard Botham was summed up at one of the Indian Cricket Board's Jubilee parties where a high-ranking Indian official commented on the incredible publicity campaign that had accompanied Muhammad Ali on his recent visit to Bombay. There were posters all over the city announcing Ali's exhibition bout which screamed: 'Come and See The Greatest''. The Indian cricketing official remarked, 'The only thing incorrect on the poster was that they had the wrong person – it should have been Mr Iron Bottom!'

Taylor's patience and Stevenson's lusty hitting brought us a lead of 54 which we had never dared anticipate the previous afternoon. The second time round Sunil Gavaskar confirmed his ranking as a Test batsman who would qualify as an opener for a World XI. He now showed us what a great technician he can be, displaying a superb technique particularly in his judgement of when to leave alone deliveries that were swinging away.

His cool-headed batting was not totally infectious with his colleagues. India caved in once more against Botham and Lever.

Sunil had managed to make 24 out of a score of 56 for 5 and by the end of the third day the jubilee Test had become more of a funeral occasion for the Indians, with them finishing on 148 for 8, only 94 runs in the lead.

Botham was the first to appreciate just how much assistance he had received from Lever whose 2 for 64 in 19 overs did no justice at all to his endeavours. Even Botham had to admit that his stamina had waned in the final session, not surprisingly as he had bowled the unbelievable number of 24 overs in succession.

Ian was back at work quickly the next morning, dismissing Yadav with his loosener almost before the crowd had settled in their seats.

Once more his greatest ally had been Taylor, who now equalled the world record for the most catches in a Test. His nine victims put him on a par with Australia's Gil Langley, who took eight catches and pulled off one stumping against England at Lord's back in 1956.

We were all delighted for Taylor because he had never played in India before. He is a total professional in his quiet and determined approach to both his batting and wicketkeeping. I've also always admired the way he trains and looks after himself, and realize more than most England players how patiently he accepted his part as understudy to Alan Knott in the early 1970s.

It hadn't always gone well for Bob in Australia so it must have given him special pleasure to equal those wicketkeeping records in Bombay. But still the talk was of the 'Ian Botham show' because Botham had broken yet another record – beating Gary Sobers and joining the élite who have taken 10 wickets and scored a century in the same Test twice.

There was to be one more umpiring incident before England recorded their comfortable 10-wicket victory with more than a day to spare. Boycott had made 11 and the total was 14 when Kapil Dev appealed for what he thought was a leg-side catch, Rao's index finger shooting up promptly as Geoff followed the ball. A huge roar erupted from the crowd, who believed Boycott was out, but the umpire had raised his arm and put it down so quickly that few people had noticed him giving Geoff out. Geoff turned his back to the umpire and carried on preparing for the next ball. The bowler looked surprised and downhearted as he trudged back to his mark. Apparently Rao informed him that the ball had been deflected off the pads! So Boycott survived and, with Gooch, saw us home with ease.

Rao's instant style of giving a batsman in or out prompted more dressing-room conversation and I felt that it was a fair criticism of the Indian umpires that they tended to react with undue haste instead of taking their time and analysing critical decisions.

We were able to enjoy a day off, for once reflecting on victory instead of defeat and it made us forget for a few hours the disappointments of Australia.

GOLDEN JUBILEE TEST v. INDIA

Played at Bombay, 15–20 February 1980. **England won by 10 wickets.**

INDIA

	First innings		Second innings	
S. M. Gavaskar	c Taylor b Botham	49	c Taylor b Botham	24
R. M. Binny	run out	15	lbw b Botham	0
D. B. Vengsarkar	c Taylor b Stevenson	34	lbw b Lever	10
*G. R. Viswanath	b Lever	11	c Taylor b Botham	5
S. M. Patil	c Taylor b Botham	30	lbw b Botham	0
Yashpal Sharma	lbw b Botham	21	lbw b Botham	27
Kapil Dev	c Taylor b Botham	0	(8) not out	45
†S. M. H. Kirmani	not out	40	(7) c Gooch b Botham	0
K. D. Ghavri	c Taylor b Stevenson	11	c Brearley b Lever	5
Shivlal Yadav	c Taylor b Botham	8	c Taylor b Botham	15
D. R. Doshi	c Taylor b Botham	6	c and b Lever	0
Extras	(B5, LB3, NB9)	17	(B4, LB8, W1, NB5)	18
Total		242		149

Fall of wickets: 1–56, 2–102, 3–108, 4–135, 5–160, 6–160, 7–181, 8–197, 9–223, 10–242.

1–4, 2–22, 3–31, 4–31, 5–56, 6–58, 7–102, 8–115, 9–148, 10–149.

ENGLAND

	First innings		Second innings	
G. A. Gooch	c Kirmani b Ghavri	8	not out	49
G. Boycott	c Kirmani b Binny	22	not out	43
W. Larkins	lbw b Ghavri	0		
D. I. Gower	lbw b Kapil Dev	16		
*J. M. Brearley	lbw b Kapil Dev	5		
I. T. Botham	lbw b Ghavri	114		
†R. W. Taylor	lbw b Kapil Dev	43		
J. F. Emburey	c Binny b Ghavri	8		
J. K. Lever	b Doshi	21		
G. B. Stevenson	not out	27		
D. L. Underwood	b Ghavri	1		
Extras	(B8, LB9, NB14)	31	(B3, LB1, NB2)	6
Total		296	(for no wkt)	98

Fall of wickets: 1–21, 2–21, 3–45, 4–57, 5–58, 6–229, 7–245, 8–262, 9–283, 10–296.

BOWLING

ENGLAND	*O*	*M*	*R*	*W*	*O*	*M*	*R*	*W*
Lever	23	3	82	1	20.2	2	65	3
Botham	22.5	7	58	6	26	7	48	7
Stevenson	14	1	59	2	5	1	13	0
Underwood	6	1	23	0	1	0	5	0
Gooch	4	2	3	0				
INDIA								
Kapil Dev	29	8	64	3	8	2	21	0
Ghavri	20.1	5	52	5	5	0	12	0
Binny	19	3	70	1				
Doshi	23	6	57	1	6	1	12	0
Yadav	6	2	22	0	6	0	31	0
Patil					3	0	8	0
Gavaskar					1	0	4	0
Viswanath					0.3	0	4	0

9. Post-Impressions and the Future

My first close encounter with Mike Brearley was on the England Under-25 tour of Pakistan in 1966–7. He was captain of that team and enjoyed immense success as an opening batsman with some prolific scores, including one double hundred and a triple century. I had just made my début for England when I went on this tour and I had the rather inglorious bowling figures after two Tests of 1 for 172, so I viewed this tour as extremely important for my future career. I found the conditions in Pakistan extremely difficult to adapt to, and I was the least successful of the spinners on the trip. Because of this and the inadequate hotel accommodation there were times when I became most depressed, and I found Mike sympathetic and understanding and indeed most helpful during this trying period.

He left a lasting impression on me both as a captain of remarkable maturity for someone so young and as a batsman who was in his element on the slower paced wickets. He is predominantly a front-foot player and a sound driver, and relishes a battle especially against the spinners – as I've found on numerous occasions when I've played against him. Mike possesses a fine defence but at times I feel that his style of play is rather mechanical and rigid; his major problem, after being at the crease a while, is breaking out and taking the initiative away from the bowler. Perhaps it is fair to say that every run Mike gets he's had to earn, as opposed to some of the players in the England side who, I feel, possessed much greater talent and ability.

When I came to consider what had gone wrong with our much publicized and frequently criticized middle order it was interesting to note just how well the older players had done in the tests – Brearley who is thirty-seven, Boycott who is thirty-nine and Taylor who is thirty-eight. These three players exhibit strong defensive techniques, maybe because they have been brought up on a more constant routine of three-day cricket in which they have had an opportunity to build an innings. They had all played a lot of cricket before the advent of the limited-overs competitions and the introduction of the 100-overs limitation on the first innings of county championship matches. This restriction and the growing amount of instant cricket has led to it being a much harder life for the up-and-coming young batsman on the verge of Test status. Brearley, Boycott and Taylor all showed the importance of having the patience to play everything on its merits in a Test match. They were prepared to grind it out, fighting for survival and then gradually pushing the score along later when the bowlers became more tired.

Prior to leaving on the tour Mike Brearley was under extreme pressure from all quarters and much has been written and said of his batting ability and the question of whether or not he was good enough to command a place in the England side, forgetting his leadership qualities. On the tour he proved not only to his critics but, more importantly, to his fellow players, that he was more than up to the task as was reflected in his performances. I was pleased Mike decided to bat down the order on the tour thus giving our middle order more solidarity. I'm sure he would have met with much greater success had he done this more in his career.

I enjoyed the experience of batting with Mike, especially in Sydney. He is unselfish and the sort of cricketer who will always come down the wicket, say encouraging things, and offer assistance when we were in difficulty, which in my case was frequently! I remember going through some torrid spells and looking down the wicket at Mike's wry smile concealed by the helmet and thinking to myself, 'There must be easier ways to earn a living.'

Life for Brearley was that much harder than it was for anyone else in the party because of the unbelievable abuse he suffered at the hands of the Australian cricketing public. They saw him as the arch antagonist towards every proposal put forward by the Australian Cricket Board over such issues as our refusal to contest the Ashes, the wearing of coloured clothing and the use of circles. It became apparent too that there remained considerable feeling still over Australia's 5–1 defeat at the hands of the Poms the previous winter and the Australian public wanted nothing more than to see the English lose.

Because Brearley tended to be England's spokesman he was the man who was most heavily criticized. The backlash seemed to be directed at him to such an extent that there were occasions when he was booed, slow handclapped and jeered at in the nastiest way often from the moment he walked from the dressing-room until he reached the crease. On the large test arenas around Australia that can be a long time in which to be so publicly harangued. As a joke at Melbourne we all held back when we went out to field so Mike could take the full brunt of abuse from the crowd. Needless to say the Melbourne crowd obliged in true fashion. Everybody playing Test cricket must accept a certain amount of barracking but the treatment of the England captain was downright boorish. The Australians looked upon Brearley with his sea-captain's beard grown before the tour as some stubborn Ayatollah. I probably receive as much abuse as anyone, being an outfielder, and some of the comments made are quite amusing, but at times I do think it rather pathetic and even sad that top-flight sportsmen should be abused and insulted in the manner that they are. Quite frequently young boys do it and there they are with their autograph books at the pavilion door at the end of the day. At times it makes me wonder if I should sign them.

The Australians were critical of Mike long before the tour started because they thought he had been greedy when representing the England team by holding out for better money for the tour. He argued that English cricket was doing the Australian game a special favour by undertaking what was a ridiculously congested programme of Test cricket, one-day internationals and an inadequate number of four-day matches. Mike stood out for the players in trying to obtain a better overall deal. In the end the players received £6,500 plus £200 for each previous tour the players had undertaken. The TCCB had also had their fair share of problems with the Australian Board in coming to an agreement as to what guarantee they should receive from the tour. In fact, just prior to the tour, there was a certain amount of doubt whether or not the tour would take place. In the end I believe the TCCB accepted a reduced guarantee and benefited more from the Jubilee Test in India than they did from the whole tour of Australia.

The Australians may not rate Mike as a player but they recognised at the end of the tour what a marvellous job he did for us when so many of our well-known batsmen were letting us down. It came as a sobering thought that apart from Botham's century at Melbourne, Boycott's 99 at Perth and Gower's 98 at Sydney, Brearley and Gooch were the only players who twice got past 50 in three Test matches, and to be fair to Gooch he played only four Test innings.

In no way should anyone think that Mike is a weak man. He is not frightened to speak up when he thinks something isn't being done the right way. I thought he was particularly good when it came to the pre-Test discussion on tactics and his analysis of the opposition; he never failed to remember those players who hadn't quite made the side. I always remember him dealing most forcibly with a television camera crew who had stationed themselves right by our dressing-room door at the Melbourne Cricket Ground. They hurriedly disappeared after the Captain explained that it was the only place on the ground where we could have some privacy. One of Mike's pet hates, I think, was photographers who were endlessly lurking around in an effort to get an exclusive photograph and it became a standing joke between us whenever we saw anyone with a camera to utter in unison, 'No, no' or 'One more, one more'. He is strong under that calm and relaxed outward appearance.

Mike also examined very thoroughly the reasons why our middle order continually collapsed in the Tests. He appreciated the problems of the younger players who had to keep adjusting from the demands of the 55-overs game to Test cricket. Peter Willey, Gower, Randall and, to a lesser extent, Larkins, were affected by poor preparation for the Test matches. This group comprises naturally gifted shot-makers who have been reared in an era when they have had to take so many risks because of the abundance of one-day cricket around the world. Willey, who did well in World Series Cup games, found himself being caught frequently in the slip cordon area in the Tests.

Brearley is a sympathetic captain who goes out of his way to analyse the different characters that make up his team. I always remember him writing in one of his books that I lacked confidence in altering the field; I prefer to play what I call a holding game and like to keep men up so that I can bowl a maiden and maintain the pressure on a batsman even if the wicket is not conducive to my type of bowling. Referring to the Old Trafford Test against Australia in 1977 he commented in his book that

> 'several times we had mutual hesitations about the appropriate field. When he has to depart from orthodoxy, Derek is surprisingly uncertain for so great a bowler. At those times it is tempting for the captain to take over. I remember feeling sorry for Derek once or twice in India as he stood covered in sweat and dust at the back of his run-up, feet turned and trousers sagging like a cricketing Chaplin, while

Greig directed fielders this way and that. But when I became captain I could also see how Greig felt if he didn't take charge completely; the ship would be quite directionless. I was prepared to risk moments of indecisiveness for the sake of involving Derek more in the strategy. Technically the problems are interesting. A left-arm slow bowler coming over the wicket usually needs a slip, a mid-off, extra cover and square cover on the off side. On the leg side he must have a backward square leg, deepish but not right out for the mis-hit sweep. He needs a short leg and a mid-on; one other fielder must be behind square on the leg side either at short leg or back twenty yards for the batsman who is looking to sweep.'

I think Mike is being pretty fair when he says I dislike parting from orthodoxy. If possible I like to maintain orthodox fields as I have great faith and belief in tried and tested field placings when they've proved successful. Perhaps I should be a little more flexible with different fields for different players. Ian Chappell, for instance, always looks to dominate from the word go and detests men up round the bat especially the man up close on the off side, as does Greg Chappell. I found it most interesting bowling to McCosker and Laird. To McCosker I couldn't bowl too straight and always aimed to bowl off stump and just outside as he is such a strong on-side player. To Laird I aimed to bowl quite a bit slower and flighted the ball more as I felt he liked to use the pace of the ball in deflecting for ones and twos.

In the main, when bowling to players of international class, I feel they don't have basic weaknesses but basic strengths; by avoiding their strengths one can often impart a superiority. That is why I like to make batsmen play the ball to the area I want them to and by having orthodox fields it is easier to achieve this. I prefer to bowl to a containing field with a circle of fielders saving one, plus of course my two or three men up round the bat. Obviously, one would have a man back on the square leg boundary for the infamous Ian Chappell sweep. In other words, I'm saying to the batsman, if you're going to get it past these fielders, you've got to play an attacking shot. In the Second Test at Sydney I remember bowling against Hughes who plays me well. He had just come in and was still to score, yet we had a long-off on the fence. Perhaps Hughes, seeing this man back, might have gone for the drive or pushed hard at the ball to get off the mark thus leading to his downfall but so far I'm not accustomed as perhaps I should be to this sort of strategy. I'm still learning, that's for sure!

I like to have men up round the bat, with a slip, a conventional bat-pad and Both's position of bat-pad on the off side. I much prefer the batsman to play defensively. Nothing is more frustrating than trying to attack the batsman and finding he gets away from you because of defensive field placings on the ring. It's much easier keeping men up round the bat on English wickets which are slower. In Australia the ball comes onto the bat far more quickly.

I thought at times that Mike was a bit quick in pushing men back instead of sticking with the holding policy. On the other hand, at no stage did we have runs on the board to play with. If one is starting out with a policy of trying to get batsmen out, the last thing in the world you want to see is the ball crashing into the fence for four. We never had big totals behind us in the Test series, only once getting past 300, and that was at Melbourne after we had already lost the series. What a difference it would have made if once or twice we had been able to bowl at Australia having run up a score of 400 or 450.

All the bowlers were affected by this problem of defending modest totals and we were too often employed to do a blocking-up job, aiming to hold them, as opposed to making a thrust for victory. Only very infrequently could I have a spell where I was genuinely attacking and I appreciated that it made it that much harder for the captain to work out his tactics.

For instance, on the fourth morning of the Second Test in Sydney when Australia were in with a good chance and had 9 wickets standing, Mike said to me, 'You'll have to keep it tight,' and it was difficult striking the balance between bowling positively and restricting the Australians from picking up runs.

I know that Mike understood my ideas about my 'holding approach' and my reluctance to see men being put back into defensive fielding positions which widened the scoring gaps, though there have been times in the past when I've liked captains to set my fields for me. Basically I need to concentrate a great deal, becoming totally wrapped up in my bowling and constantly worrying about the length, the line, and the flight, the essential principles all bowlers must follow. Such aspects as moving fielders here and there can interrupt my rhythm. To be fair to Mike I hadn't played under his captaincy since 1977 in the Home series against the Australians. Perhaps he was still assessing such things as whether a man should be a bit finer in a certain fielding position, or whether to move fielders because runs were coming too quickly in one area. He had had little experience of captaining me in first-class matches or of seeing me bowl for long periods and this must have counted against him in not knowing the vulnerable areas in which I was going to be scored off.

What Mike was very good at was putting the best fielders in key positions such as mid-wicket and cover. Because we had such brilliant fielders as Gower and Randall we could afford to have mid-off and mid-on back a little bit because both these two were capable of covering so much ground.

Lever and Larkins almost came into this category too with Mike being able to have someone like Ned in a fairly straight position at extra cover. This was a great help to all the bowlers.

I wanted to keep men up round the bat as long as possible because I was usually in with a better chance of getting someone out caught close in than I was if someone were driving at the ball and perhaps being caught at extra cover or mid-wicket. Those sort of dismissals I regarded as a bonus.

Traditionally the captain has to shoulder the blame when a Test series is lost. Automatically he's the man who is accused of doing things the wrong way. People see it as his tour, his show. But I do not think Mike could have approached the captaincy any differently, particularly once we had suffered the enormous blow of Mike Hendrick having to fly home injured before the First Test.

Australia outplayed us and one or two players on our side felt they could have done better; we certainly ought to have been capable of saving the First Test at Perth and I sensed that we could even have won the Test at Sydney against the odds, if we had had the breaks and made another 50–60 runs in our second innings. The sort of break that I'm thinking of was our unanimous appeal for a catch behind the stumps when Greg Chappell had hardly got going. We played badly at Melbourne but I felt that in the circumstances we were a good enough side to have gone down either 2–1 or 1–0.

Australia had the advantage of being more geared up for Test matches because they had their three Tests against the West Indians interspersed with our series. They were more in the groove for Test cricket than we were; we tended to have the one-day game on our minds. The one-day internationals did not seem to be as detrimental to Australia.

It also said a lot for Brearley's standing as a captain that after we'd been beaten so comprehensively by the Australians we managed to win the jubilee Test comfortably in India. It showed that the team still wanted to succeed for him and was a reflection of the excellent spirit that existed despite our results.

I have been a member of far more successful England sides, and yet haven't always enjoyed the atmosphere. My biggest complaint about this tour was the pressure of the travelling, the unbelievable number of internal flights and the constant switching of hotels, which had us waking up and not being sure whether we were in Adelaide, Melbourne or Sydney! But that was hardly Brearley's fault.

Mike demonstrated that he knew just when to impose a degree of discipline and this was underlined after we had spent four days in the luxurious Wrest Point Casino Hotel at Hobart. Mike called the team together and said, 'You've had your fun, now we've got to get down to playing cricket.' This was the strong side of Mike coming out, and the players got the message. Mike took a certain amount of leg-pulling but confirmed for me that he was well capable of handling the lads in relaxed moments off the field as well as in dire situations in a Test match. He knew when to be firm and might be heard tactfully saying to a couple of young players in the dressing-room, 'You'll learn more from watching the cricket than reading those books.' He could make a point without shouting or giving anyone an embarrassing dressing-down.

Younger players in the side over the last two years have the highest respect for him. He's helped them considerably and nobody pays higher tributes to the captain than Botham. Nobody can take away his impressive record as Captain of England over the years.

I understand that Mike stood out for me during that seven-hour selection meeting when the 1979–80 tour party was being discussed. He has always had a great respect for me as a bowler and it drew me even closer to him and made me want to get wickets for him. I dearly wanted him to do well with the bat.

Throughout the Packer affair he had been particularly sympathetic to my case. He knew how torn I had been about sacrificing my career as an England bowler. On one occasion he went out of his way to come and talk to me in the second season of WSC when England were also in Australia.

It meant a tremendous amount to me when Brearley came round to the World XI's hotel and spent more than two hours discussing the England tour and what was happening in our cricketing world with WSC. It showed an understanding towards someone with whom he had played for so many years and that I had not been forgotten by my England team-mates.

Also, where the WSC business was concerned Mike was opposed to what it stood for but he did not take it to a personal level, which I sensed was the case with some England players in the earlier Packer days. The attitude of one or two England players at the outset of WSC had been hurtful. They didn't seem to understand that I was only trying to do the best for my wife and children.

There were other people in cricket who talked about my throwing away the opportunity of one day breaking the world Test wickets record. There never seemed to be any point in my attempting to explain that taking a record number of wickets is no guarantee that the bills are being paid! However, I felt that Brearley was more sympathetic about the motives that led people to sign for WSC.

If there were few encouraging aspects about our batting setting aside Boycott, Gooch and Brearley in the Tests and Peter Willey in the one-day internationals, then our bowling didn't exactly bring the roof down either. We had to accept the loss of the Derbyshire pair, Mike Hendrick and Geoff Miller.

I felt that Graham Dilley gained a lot of valuable experience and would have returned more encouraging figures but for a nagging side injury towards the end of the tour which cut him down quite a bit. He has a fine flowing high action and an enormous amount of potential to become a genuine quick Test bowler.

One had to appreciate that Dilley had appeared in only twenty-odd first-class matches and was very raw when the tour began. He had never experienced a full day in the field and there he was being thrust in at the deep end. He is aware that he needs to build up his stamina and probably do some weight training as his body fills out. He put in a lot of work in attending Gillingham Football Club's training sessions when we returned from Australia after the tour. His ability to be fierce for a short spell served us well in the one-day games.

Brearley suggested to me that Kent would be better advised in the future to regard Dilley as a shock bowler who ought to be worked in short spells. Realizing we had unearthed someone a bit different, we were perhaps inclined to over-bowl him in his first full season with the county.

Again, Brearley could see Dilley being employed in a slightly different rôle in one-day matches, concentrating on length and line and not worrying so much about that extra yard of pace. We had to remember on tour that Dilley was still only twenty and it was encouraging that he revealed himself as a young bowler prepared to listen and digest the knowledge of people like Bob Willis and Botham. He has had a lot of people advising him about his run-up, his action, and where his left foot should be pointing after his delivery stride. What is important is that he has the natural gift of simply bowling fast.

At a time when England desperately need to find the next generation of Test pace bowlers to succeed Bob, Hendrick and Chris Old in the 1980s Dilley surely has the Test cricketing world at his feet.

He is shy and retiring off the field but he impressed England players and the opposition with his aggression and that essential mean instinct which should be a part of every fast bowler's armoury. He does not mind hitting the batsmen and could easily become England's number one strike bowler in the next two or three years.

Bob Willis, who kept urging Dilley on in a very unselfish manner, is different in style and approach being much more of an effort bowler. Like me he found it a major problem not being able to bowl long spells in between the Tests and seemed to have lost the pace that made him our principal fast bowler in the 1970s following the retirement of John Snow.

Graham Stevenson became a most popular member of the tour party because of his enthusiasm on the field and his sense of fun off it. I would like to see someone of more pace using the new ball but he could become a useful third seamer and has the ability to play an important innings late in the order as he proved on his Test début in Bombay. Lever confirmed how useful it is to have a left-arm fast bowler to back up the right armers, and Stevenson was probably under-used in the Tests and the one-day internationals. He is a marvellous team man and has the added virtue, unlike most fast bowlers, of never breaking down.

With Hendrick going home enormous responsibility fell on Botham's shoulders. Typically he accepted it as another challenge and thought nothing of bowling unchanged for two hours, often in uncomfortable heat. Few Test bowlers can swing the ball as he can either way and he has that aggressive instinct that makes him come in that much stronger if he has just been hit for four. He can pull out the extra quick delivery and can be really nasty with his bouncer. Nor does he readily hold back against tail-end batsmen because he can bat so well and it never worries him if they want to bowl short at him in return.

Brearley used Dilley sparingly at Sydney and treated Bob Willis in much the same way in Melbourne. There was always the temptation to keep going back to Botham because of his reputation for being able to break an important stand and to take wickets when no one else threatened to do so. By his own high standards Botham was probably a little disappointing at Sydney and at Melbourne and must have suffered through being overworked. It also meant that it took a toll on his batting. He was all too often padding up in the midst of another middle-order collapse an hour or so after he had finished bowling and this was something that the younger England players had not encountered in the previous three years.

Magnificent all-rounder though he obviously is (in Brearley's opinion only the great Gary Sobers has been better) I believe that Botham is a better bowler than batsman. The way he bats he leaves himself open, taking as many risks as he does. Some of the shots he attempts early on in an innings may be very bold and none of us are surprised if he drives or pulls the second or third ball out of the ground for six.

His theory – and he makes it work in practice – is that the best form of defence is attack. He hates being restricted and with characteristic impetuosity wants to register his authority straight away over every bowler.

I just have the feeling that unlike Ian the really great batsmen, the top flight quality players, settle themselves in for twenty or thirty minutes and build their large Test innings from there. But this is mild criticism of someone who is so gifted, plays so many shots, hits the ball frighteningly hard and who has already made five Test centuries, all by the age of twenty-four. It would be wrong to curb Botham's natural attacking game.

In any age of cricket he would have been sensational but in the modern era shares the attitude of so many younger players who have been forced to bat more loosely because of the demands of one-day cricket.

When I come to analyse my own bowling contribution in the Test matches I have to relate to what was going on, or rather what wasn't going on between the Tests. I am sure my bowling suffered through long periods of inactivity between the major matches. For example, between the First and Second Tests I did not deliver a single first-class over as I was restricted to 19 overs in the one-day internationals.

There was another period between the Second Test and the match against New South Wales when eighteen days went by without my getting any cricket in the middle. I am the kind of bowler who needs to find his rhythm through long spells and the preparation for the five day matches was quite inadequate for me. My consolation and a source of some satisfaction when looking back at my thirteen Test victims was that only leg spinner Jim Higgs did not bat from one to five, and I'm referring to someone of Hughes's quality batting at five. Overall, I felt that my Test record compared favourably with my efforts on both the 1970–71 and 1974–5 tours.

Geoff Boycott was rarely out of the news on tour. He was the only batsman who scored over a thousand runs but would have been a bit disappointed with his test match form after his defiant unbeaten 99 at Perth. Time and again he held our batting together and was very much the main stay in the World Series Cup games.

What a pity he had such a tendency to attract unfavourable publicity through his ill-chosen comments and often ill-timed off-the-field incidents. For instance, on the eve of the first Test he was involved in a petulant exchange of words with the captain during our net practice. Brearley had asked Boycott to have a look at the wicket and to give some advice on what he ought to do if he won the toss.

England's senior batsman turned on him and was reported as saying, 'I haven't had a look and I won't be. I won't be fielding in the slips and taking your catches so there is no need for me to say what I think. I've given advice before and it hasn't been taken, so bugger it.' What was interesting about this feud at the nets was that Brearley later made no attempt to hush up the details when confronted by the media about what had happened. Some pressmen had the impression that the captain was so annoyed at being rebuffed that he wasn't going to try and cover up the fact to protect Boycott.

The first indication that Boycott was suffering from a mood of discontent was around the time of the first one-day international when he was left out of the side. He had been clearly disappointed when not invited to act as one of the selectors during the tour and now there was brooding resentment that he was being unfairly done down.

No one can deny that Geoff is a world-class opening batsman but he is a mighty complex man. I was never quite sure whether some of his rather pertinent comments were simply his brand of dry Yorkshire humour or whether they were meant in deadly earnest. I shall always remember a typical Boycott comment in an early tour discussion with the captain when he said with a wry smile on his face, 'With your brains and my ability we have got to do well on this tour!'

He is basically so egotistically minded about his cricket that he gives the impression that his own performance matters far more than the end result. He isn't particularly interested in watching the game once he is out and always seems geared up for only two things: his batting and his reputation. With his enormous experience he obviously has a lot of good ideas to offer but somehow he finds it hard to put them across. He may be intolerant of his fellow professionals but he would have so much to contribute to younger players if he could get closer to them off the field. However, away from the cricket Boycott appeared to prefer his own company and usually had a single room in the hotels that we stayed in. I thought it was sad that he didn't want to be more involved with the team between playing and that he chose to cut himself off and lead his own life.

I spent some time trying to convince Geoff that he was all right to play in the first of the one-day finals against the West Indies at Melbourne when he was complaining about a finger bruised a few days before during the Sydney Test. I had lunched with him and in our discussion it was obvious that he was still brooding about being dropped from the first of the one-day games against the West Indies when Brearley had opened in his place.

Sometimes Geoff gives the impression that he believes other players think he cannot play; it is almost a lack of confidence in his own ability.

Gooch, who makes everyone laugh when imitating the actions of his fellow England players, took off Geoff's accent almost perfectly, ribbing the great Yorkshire batsman with such comments as, 'I'm the greatest player in the world,' or telling Geoff that nobody could count to six so well, referring to Geoff's habit of pinching the strike at the end of the over.

Boycott certainly had an uncanny habit of saying the wrong things at the wrong time. Comments made, apparently off the record, to a freelance reporter engaged with ITN's television team back-fired terribly.

The television interviewer's article appeared in the *Sunday Telegraph* and was immediately quoted back to Australia. The paper reported Boycott as saying, 'They'd have me out there on one leg if it suited them. I tell the selectors that I'm not fit, and they don't listen, they are taking it out on me because no one else can get any runs. They took the vice captaincy from me, then removed me from the selection panel. You'd think I didn't know anything about cricket, wouldn't you? I play best when I'm surrounded by people who appreciate me. I'm just fed up with the whole set-up.'

Alec Bedser was obliged to call a full-blown press conference in order to resolve the latest Boycott rumpus. The manager was as diplomatic as he could be in trying to calm down the situation. Commenting on Boycott's attitude on tour he said that Boycott had admitted to him that there were occasions when things got on top of him and when that happened he was inclined to 'blow his top'. Bedser commented, 'I think, as he admitted himself, that there is the odd occasion when he gets depressed and then he is inclined, as he put it, to flare up.'

There had been a forty-minute meeting in Sydney after our arrival from Melbourne between Bedser, the captain and Boycott; Bedser was at pains to stress that 'Boycott's overall attitude had been good. I think that would be a very fair thing to say. He says he has been very happy on this tour.'

The manager went to great lengths, too, to play down another contretemps between the captain and Boycott before the start of the first of the World Series Cup finals in Melbourne. Bedser stated that when he and Brearley had walked on to the Melbourne Cricket Ground they had asked Boycott how he felt. Geoff had replied that he was not one hundred per cent fit but he would play if the management wanted him to. 'I said we do,' Bedser said. In resolving an incident which hadn't done morale much good, Bedser touched on the unfortunate dressing-room palaver before the Second Test in Sydney when Geoff had refused to play. About that episode Bedser commented, 'Geoff didn't consider he was one hundred per cent fit. You can't say he was happy to play there because he wasn't happy to play yesterday' (referring to Melbourne). There was even a humorous conclusion to Geoff's publicly aired grievances, with the rest of the team all signing a card to him which bore the words, 'We all love you Geoff'.

Whatever one said about Geoff and his much publicized disagreements with the management, there was no doubt that younger players could have learned a great deal from his dedication to his job as an opening batsman.

Gooch appeared to have learned most from him and became his most successful partner. He does not possess Geoff's defensive technique and likes to hit the ball in the air and may still possibly be better suited batting at number three or four in future.

David Gower found the game harder than at any time in his meteoric rise to Test fame. He was suddenly confronted with the best pace attack in the world against the West Indies and learned that someone like Lillee is in another class from most of the Test fast bowlers he has encountered since making his spectacular début for England two years ago.

Gower has a tendency to get out in some horrific ways but underneath it all is the most gifted stroke player among our younger brigade of batsmen. Possibly he is still trying to discover his minor limitations. People suggested that David didn't care because of his casual manner and expression of indifference when he walked back to the pavilion. But his depressing and erratic form worried him considerably behind that cool and calm outward appearance. It is refreshing in some ways to see a young batsman like him who wants to play his shots and it was typical of him when he went in to bat at Bombay with Ghavri on a possible hat-trick. Vishwanath had put a man back for the hook and Ghavri tried to bounce Gower first ball. It didn't get up as much as he expected but Gower still hit it for four. That's the way he plays; he takes risks but he is so exciting to watch, and one could argue that there is room for anyone who can average a century in every third Test, although it would be nice to see him getting the 40s and 50s in between.

The West Indies certainly dominated the season in Australia and one man stood out above everyone: Viv Richards, whom I rate as the best on-side player the world has ever seen. I cannot recall another batsman hitting the ball through mid-wicket and mid-on with so much ease, and he is a good hooker too.

We evolved a plan towards the end of the tour in trying to contain the great man by bowling more at the off stump and outside on a full length. It worked to an extent but Viv's footwork is so good that he still made big scores off us.

Dennis Lillee and the other Australian fast bowlers were convinced that our line of approach made no difference; they thought Viv's off-side play had improved incredibly from the year before when we were playing WSC. They no longer regarded it as his weakness.

If the batting of Viv, the impeccable Gordon Greenidge, and Alvin Kallicharran gave them their big totals then the real dominance of the West Indians was driven home in the World Series Cup and in their 2–0 Test success over Australia by their combination of four fast bowlers. They had the perfect blend, starting with Michael Holding who is inclined to bowl straight and amazingly fast in his opening spell, then slowing down a bit when brought back. 'Big Bird' Joel Garner made the ball bounce more than anyone else because of his extraordinary height, while Colin Croft used the crease cleverly, making it come into you, all the time, and was their most improved bowler. Then they had Andy Roberts who can still be superb with his swing and variation of pace. It may be sad for the purists to see a team being so dependent on pace but the West Indies could argue that it was effective, especially for one-day cricket.

My final reflections on the Australians were that they had been moulded into a very competent Test team with the return of their W S C players and it was pleasing to see that there was no friction or problems between the W S C men and the new breed of Australian Test cricketers who had developed when Packer signed up the cream of the country's cricket talent three years earlier. It probably helped them integrate well with people like Border, Dymock and Hughes playing such important parts in their success against us.

Like the West Indies, Australia were almost totally reliant on pace bowling and were lucky that Lillee bowled so magnificently whether with the new ball or when coming back to use the old ball. As one of the truly great fast bowlers of any period of Test cricket it would be wonderful for the English cricketing public, who have not seen him for five years, if he can return in the Centenary Test in August 1980.

I thought Greg Chappell was very much the key to Australia's batting; he was the man most likely to make a big 100 in the Tests and was the person we most wanted to see the back of.

Looking to the future I should love to think I can keep bowling well enough to stay in the England team. Sometimes it is hard not to think about Lance Gibb's world record of 309 Test wickets and the English record of 307 held by Fred Trueman, especially when all sorts of people who follow the game come up and ask you what it feels like to be chasing those targets

During the tests in Australia I slipped past Bishen Bedi's total of 266 and at the time of writing need another 22 wickets for my 300th in Test cricket.

I never realized that my bowling career was so closely followed thousands of miles from the grounds of Kent and England until an avid Indian cricket-lover with the delightful name of Mr Mama introduced himself to me during the jubilee test in Bombay, having previously written to me in Australia. He had compiled an incredible statistical breakdown of my 278 Test victims, all logged in chronological order, going back to Headingly in 1966 when I took my first Test wicket (that of Rohan Kanhai). Mr Mama has recorded the details of every wicket, how I dismissed my opponents and the number of times I've got them out in Test matches. I shall treasure his statistical endeavours as long as I live and have, with his permission, recorded them in this book.

Just one regret hangs over my return to the England team after what so many people described as my 'defection' to WSC and that was the fact that my father, Leslie Frank Underwood, died before he could see me wearing the England sweater once again. He loved his cricket and was immensely proud of my achievements, encouraging me tremendously. When I joined WSC he didn't say a lot but I learned from my mother that he had definite reservations and deep down he thought that I might have done the wrong thing. He did not discuss it and

I think it hurt him that I had, in his eyes, turned my back on English cricket and what it meant to him. He would have dearly loved to live a little longer if he had known I was going to come back and play Test cricket once more for my country.

England's tour and Test averages (Australia 1979–80)

TOUR BATTING

	M.	Inns	N.O.	H.S.	Agg.	Ave.
G. Gooch	6	12	2	115	582	58.20
G. Boycott	7	13	3	110	534	53.40
G. Miller	4	6	2	71	203	50.75
G. Dilley	5	6	3	38*	101	33.67
M. Brearley	6	10	1	81	297	33.00
P. Willey	6	12	3	101*	269	29.89
I. Botham	5	8	1	119*	209	29.86
D. Gower	8	14	2	98*	338	28.16
D. Randall	6	10	–	97	250	25.00
W. Larkins	5	9	1	90	190	23.75
G. Stevenson	3	4	1	33	64	21.33
J. Emburey	2	3	–	50	63	21.00
R. Taylor	7	10	1	47*	184	20.44
J. Lever	6	6	2	22	54	13.50
D. Underwood	5	7	–	43	67	12.43
D. Bairstow	2	2	–	12	13	6.50
R. Willis	4	6	–	11	21	3.50
M. Hendrick	1	1	–	1	1	1.00

* Denotes not out.

TOUR BOWLING

	O.	M.	R.	W	Ave.
I. Botham	193.1	67	426	21	20.29
D. Underwood	253	80	581	25	23.24
G. Stevenson	68	11	235	9	26.11
G. Dilley	88.1	11	243	7	34.71
G. Gooch	41	11	110	3	36.67
J. Lever	192.4	50	475	12	39.58
J. Emburey	111.2	25	282	7	40.29
P. Willey	111	17	332	7	47.43
G. Miller	106	20	268	5	53.60
R. Willis	129	30	252	3	84.00
G. Boycott	4	—	19	—	—
W. Larkins	6	—	15	—	—
M. Hendrick	4	1	14	—	—

TEST BATTING

	M.	Inns	N.O.	H.S.	Agg.	Ave.
G. Gooch	2	4	–	99	172	43.00
G. Dilley	2	4	2	38*	80	40.00
I. Botham	3	6	1	119*	187	37.40
G. Boycott	3	6	1	99*	176	35.20
M. Brearley	3	6	1	64	171	34.20
D. Gower	3	6	1	98*	152	30.40
R. Taylor	3	6	–	32	102	17.00
J. Lever	1	2	–	22	34	17.00
G. Miller	1	2	–	25	33	16.50
W. Larkins	1	2	–	25	28	14.00
D. Underwood	3	6	–	43	71	11.83
D. Randall	2	4	–	25	26	6.50
P. Willey	3	6	–	12	35	5.83
R. Willis	3	6	–	11	21	3.50

* Denotes not out.

TEST BOWLING

	O	M.	R.	W.	Ave.
G. Gooch	19	6	36	2	18.00
I. Botham	173.1	62	371	19	19.53
D. Underwood	160.2	48	405	13	31.15
J. Lever	60.4	18	129	4	32.25
G. Dilley	53	5	143	3	47.67
R. Willis	114	26	224	3	74.67
G. Miller	21	2	66	—	—
P. Willey	19	2	56	—	—

Appendix 1. Derek Underwood: A Statistical Portrait

compiled by B. B. Mama

Underwood's 278 Scalps in 78 Tests

Test no.	Series	Centre	Victim no.	Batsmen out & how				1st Inns	2nd Inns
		( ) = 10wM		*( ) = Batting Order (Top Six)*	*o = Dismissed for 'duck'*				*→ = 5wI*
1	1966 v. WI	Nottingham			Nil			0–5	0–86
2		Leeds	1	(3)	Kanhai	Ct–f		1–81	
3	1967 v. Pak	Nottingham	2	(5)	Hanif	Ct–f		1–17	
			3	(3)	Saeed	Ct–f			
			4	(6)	Mushtaq	LBW	o		
			5		Majid	Ct–f			
			6		Intikhab	Ct–w/k			
			7		Bari	Ct–f			→ 5–52
4		Oval			Nil			0–12	
			8		Mushtaq	Ct–f			
			9		Burki	Bowled	o		2–48
5	1968 v. Aus	Lord's	10	(2)	Redpath	Bowled			
			11	(4)	Walters	Bowled			2–8
6		Birmingham	12	(5)	Walters	Ct & B			
			13	(6)	Sheahan	Bowled			
			14		Gleeson	Ct–f		3–48	0–14
7		Leeds	15	(4)	Walters	Ct–f			
			16		Freeman	Bowled			
			17		McKenzie	LBW			
			18		Connolly	Ct–f		4–41	
			19	(5)	I. Chappell	Ct–f			
			20		Gleeson	Ct–w/k			2–52
8		Oval	21		Gleeson	Ct–f			
			22		Connolly	Bowled		2–89	
			23	(2)	Inverarity	LBW			
			24	(3)	Redpath	LBW			
			25	(4)	I. Chappell	LBW			
			26	(5)	Walters	Ct–w/k			
			27		McKenzie	Ct–f	o		
			28		Mallett	Ct–f	o		
			29		Gleeson	Bowled			→ 7–50

Test no.	Series	Centre	Victim no.		Batsmen out & how			1st Inns	2nd Inns
9	1968 v. Pak	Lahore	30		Majid	Ct–f		1–36	
			31	(2)	Gul	Ct–f			1–29
10		Dacca	32		Intikhab	LBW		1–45	
			33	(2)	Salahuddin	LBW			
			34	(5)	Saeed	Ct–w/k			
			35	(3)	Iqbal	Bowled			
			36	(4)	Mushtaq	Ct–f			
			37		Hanif	LBW			→ 5–94
11		Karachi			(Riot – Pak did not bat)				
12	1969 v. WI	Manchester	38		Foster	Stumped		1–15	
			39	(1)	Fredericks	Ct–f			1–31
13		Leeds	40	(2)	Camacho	Ct–f			
			41	(3)	Davis	Ct & B			
			42	(4)	Butcher	Ct–w/k			
			43		Shepherd	Ct–w/k	0		4–55
14	1969 v. NZ	Lord's (11–70)	44	(1)	Dowling	Ct–f			
			45	(5)	Pollard	Ct–f			
			46		Motz	Bowled			
			47		Hadlee	Ct–f		4–38	
			48	(3)	Congdon	Ct–f			
			49	(4)	Hastings	Ct–w/k	0		
			50	(5)	Pollard	LBW	0		
			51	(6)	Burgess	LBW			
			52		Wadsworth	Bowled			
			53		Taylor	Bowled	0		
			54		Motz	Ct–w/k			→ 7–32
15		Nottingham	55	(5)	Pollard	Ct–f		1–44	0–5
16		Oval (12–101)	56	(2)	Turner	Ct–f			
			57	(3)	Congdon	Ct–f			
			58		Taylor	Ct–f	0		
			59		Wadsworth	Ct–f			
			60		Motz	Ct–f			
			61		Cunis	Ct–f	0	→ 6–41	
			62	(1)	Murray	Ct & B			
			63	(2)	Turner	Bowled			
			64	(6)	Pollard	Ct–f			
			65		Taylor	Stumped			
			66		Motz	Ct–f			
			67		Cunis	LBW			→ 6–60
17	1970 v. Aus	Brisbane	68	(4)	Walters	Bowled			
			69	(5)	Redpath	Ct–f			
			70		Sheahan	Ct–w/k	0	3–101	
			71	(5)	Redpath	Ct & B			1–23

Test no.	Series	Centre	Victim no.	Batsmen out & how				1st Inns	2nd Inns
18		Sydney	72	(5)	G. Chappell	Ct & B			
			73	(6)	Stackpole	Ct–f			
			74		Marsh	Ct–f			
			75		Mallett	Bowled		4–66	0–17
19		Melbourne	76	(5)	Walters	Bowled		1–78	
			77	(3)	I. Chappell	Bowled			1–38
20		Adelaide	78	(1)	Stackpole	Bowled		1–45	
			79	(3)	I. Chappell	Ct–f			1–85
21		Sydney	80	(5)	Redpath	Ct & B			
			81	(6)	Walters	Stumped		2–39	
			82		Marsh	Bowled			
			83		Jenner	Ct–f			2–28
22	1970–71 v. NZ	Christchurch (12–97)	84	(1)	Dowling	Ct–f			
			85	(5)	Shrimpton	Ct–f	0		
			86	(6)	Turner	Bowled			
			87		Wadsworth	Ct–f	0		
			88		Cunis	Bowled	0		
			89		H. Howarth	Stumped	0	→ 6–12	
			90	(3)	Congdon	Bowled			
			91	(5)	Morgan	Bowled	0		
			92	(6)	Shrimpton	Ct–f			
			93	(4)	Turner	Bowled			
			94		Pollard	LBW			
			95		H. Howarth	Ct–f			→ 6–85
23		Auckland	96	(1)	Turner	Ct & B			
			97	(2)	Dowling	Ct & B			
			98	(3)	Congdon	Bowled	0		
			99	(4)	Morgan	Ct & B			
			100	(6)	Shrimpton	LBW		→ 5–108	0–0
24	1971 v. Pak	Birmingham			Nil			0–102	
25	1971 v. Ind	Oval	101		Venkat	LBW		1–49	
			102	(2)	Mankad	Ct–f			
			103	(4)	Sardesai	Ct–w/k			
			104	(6)	Solkar	Ct & B			3–72
26	1972 v. Aus	Leeds (10–82)	105	(1)	Stackpole	Ct–w/k			
			106	(4)	G. Chappell	LBW			
			107	(5)	Sheahan	Ct–f	0		
			108		Marsh	Ct–f		4–37	
			109	(1)	Stackpole	LBW			
			110	(4)	G. Chappell	Ct–f			
			111	(6)	Walters	Ct–f			
			112		Marsh	Ct–w/k			
			113		Inverarity	Ct–f	0		
			114		Lillee	Bowled			→ 6–45

Test no.	Series	Centre	Victim no.	Batsmen out & how		1st Inns	2nd Inns
27		Oval	115	(5) Edwards	Bowled		
			116	(6) Sheahan	Ct–f		
			117	Marsh	Bowled		
			118	Inverarity	Ct–f	4–90	
			119	(3) I. Chappell	Ct–f		
			120	(4) G. Chappell	LBW		2–94
28	1972–3 v. Ind	Delhi	121	(1) Gavaskar	Ct–f		
			122	(4) Sardesai	Ct–f		
			123	(5) Viswanath	Bowled		
			124	Engineer	Ct–w/k	0–16	4–56
29		Calcutta	125	(1) Gavaskar	Ct–f		
			126	Engineer	Bowled	2–43	
			127	(5) Engineer	Ct–w/k		1–36
30		Kanpur	128	(1) Chauhan	Ct–f		
			129	(6) Solkar	Bowled		
			130	Engineer	Bowled	3–90	
			131	(2) Gavaskar	Ct–f		
			132	(3) Wadekar	Ct & B		2–46
31		Bombay	133	(5) Pataudi	Bowled	1–100	
			134	(1) Engineer	Bowled		
			135	(2) Gavaskar	Ct & B		2–70
32	1972–3 v. Pak	Lahore	136	(4) Mushtaq	Bowled		
			137	(6) Intikhab	Bowled		
			138	Bari	Bowled	3–58	0–38
33		Hyderabad		Nil		0–119	
34	1973 v. NZ	Leeds		Nil		0–27	0–14
35	1973 v. WI	Oval	139	Boyce	Bowled		
			140	Inshan Ali	Ct–f	2–68	
			141	Murray	Ct–f		1–51
36		Birmingham	142	(1) Fredericks	Ct–f		
			143	Murray	Bowled		
			144	Holder	Ct–f	3–40	
			145	(4) Lloyd	Ct–w/k		
			146	(5) Kallich'rn	Bowled		2–66
37		Lord's		Nil		0–105	
38	1973–4 v. WI	Port of Spain	147	(6) Sobers	Ct–f	1–56	
			148	(3) Kallich'rn	Ct–f		
			149	(4) Lloyd	Ct–f		2–48
39		Kingston		Nil		0–98	
40		Georgetown	150	(4) Kanhai	Bowled	1–36	
41		Port of Spain	151	(6) Sobers	Bowled	0–57	1–19

Test no.	Series	Centre	Victim no.	Batsmen out & how			1st Inns	2nd Inns
42	1974 v. Ind	Manchester	152	(5) Viswanath	Bowled		1–50	
			153	(2) Solkar	Ct–f			1–45
43		Lord's	154	(4) Viswanath	Bowled		1–18	
44		Birmingham	155	Venkat	Bowled	o	1–30	0–3
45	1974 v. Pak	Leeds	156	(4) Mushtaq	Ct–f		1–26	0–0
46		Lord's	157	(3) Zaheer	Ct–f			
		(13–71)	158	(4) Mushtaq	Ct–f	o		
			159	(5) Wasim Raja	Ct–f			
			160	(6) Iqbal	Ct–f			
			161	Intikhab	Bowled		→ 5–20	
			162	(2) M. Khan	LBW			
			163	(3) Zaheer	Ct–f			
			164	(5) Wasim Raja	Ct–f			
			165	(6) Iqbal	Ct–f	o		
			166	Intikhab	Bowled	o		
			167	I. Khan	Ct–f	o		
			168	Bari	LBW			
			169	Sarfraz	Ct–f			→ 8–51
47		Oval	170	(2) M. Khan	Bowled			
			171	(3) Zaheer	Bowled		2–106	
			172	(4) Mushtaq	Bowled			1–15
48	1974–5 v. Aus	Brisbane	173	(4) G. Chappell	Ct–f			
			174	(5) Edwards	Ct–w/k		2–54	
			175	(3) I. Chappell	Ct–f			
			176	(4) G. Chappell	Bowled			2–63
49		Melbourne		Nil			0–62	0–43
50		Sydney	177	(1) Redpath	Ct–f			
			178	(4) Walters	Bowled		0–54	2–65
51		Adelaide	179	(1) Redpath	Ct–f			
		(11–215)	180	(2) McCosker	Ct–f			
			181	(3) I. Chappell	Ct–w/k	o		
			182	(4) G. Chappell	LBW			
			183	(5) Walters	Ct–f			
			184	(6) Marsh	Ct–f			
			185	Jenner	Bowled		→ 7–113	
			186	(1) Redpath	Bowled			
			187	(3) I. Chappell	Ct–w/k			
			188	(4) G. Chappell	Ct–f			
			189	(6) Marsh	Ct–f			4–102
52		Melbourne		Nil				0–39
53	1974–5 v. NZ	Auckland	190	(3) Parker	Ct–w/k			
			191	Wadsworth	LBW			
			192	Hadlee	Ct–f		3–38	
			193	(3) Congdon	Bowled			
			194	Wadsworth	Ct–f			2–47

Test no.	Series	Centre	Victim no.	Batsmen out & how			1st Inns	2nd Inns
54		Christchurch	195	(6)	G. Howarth	Bowled		
			196		H. Howarth	LBW	2–35	
55	1975 v. Aus.	Birmingham	197		Thomson	Ct–f	1–10	
56		Lord's	198		Thomson	Bowled	1–29	0–64
57		Leeds	199		Gilmour	Ct–f	1–22	
			200	(2)	Marsh	Bowled		1–40
58		Oval	201	(6)	Walters	Bowled	1—96	
			202	(3)	Edwards	Ct–f		1–5
59	1976 v. WI	Nottingham	203	(3)	Richards	Ct–f		
			204	(4)	Kallich'rn	Ct–f		
			205	(5)	Lloyd	Ct–f		
			206		Gomes	Ct–f	4–82	0–9
60		Lord's	207	(2)	Greenidge	Ct–f		
			208	(5)	Lloyd	Ct–w/k		
			209		Holding	Bowled		
			210		Holder	Ct–f		
			211		Roberts	Bowled	5–39	
			212		Gomes	Bowled		
			213		Julien	Bowled		2–73
61		Manchester	214	(2)	Greenidge	Bowled		
			215	(6)	King	Ct–f		
			216		Daniel	LBW	3–55	0–90
62		Leeds			Nil		0–80	
63		Oval	217	(4)	Rowe	Stumped		
			218		Murray	Ct & B		
			219		Holding	Bowled	3–165	0–38
64	1976–7 v. Ind	Delhi	220		Sharma	Ct–f	1–19	
			221	(1)	Gavaskar	Ct–f		
			222	(6)	M. Amarnath	Ct–f		
			223	(5)	Patel	Ct & B		
			224	(3)	Sharma	Ct–f		4–78
65		Calcutta	225	(4)	Viswanath	Ct–f	1–24	
			226	(1)	Gavaskar	Bowled		
			227		Prasanna	Ct–f		
			228		Bedi	Bowled		3–50
66		Madras	229	(5)	Patel	Bowled		
			230		Prasanna	Ct & B	2–16	
			231	(1)	Gavaskar	Ct–f		
			232	(3)	M. Amarnath	Ct–f		
			233	(4)	Viswanath	Ct–f		
			234	(5)	Prasanna	Ct–f		4–28

Test no.	Series	Centre	Victim no.	Batsmen out & how			1st Inns	2nd Inns
67		Bangalore	235	(4) Viswanath	Ct–f		1–45	
			236	(1) Gavaskar	Ct–f			
			237	(4) Patel	Ct–w/k			
			238	(5) Yajurvindra	Ct–f			
			239	Kirmani	Ct–f			4–76
68		Bombay	240	(1) Gavaskar	Ct & B			
			241	(3) S. Amarnath	Bowled			
			242	Kirmani	Ct–w/k			
			243	Prasanna	Bowled		4–89	
			244	(1) Gavaskar	Ct–f			
			245	(2) Gaekwad	Stumped			
			246	(4) Patel	Ct–f			
			247	Kirmani	Ct–f			
			248	Ghavri	Ct–f			→ 5–84
69	1976–7 v. Aus	Melbourne	249	(4) G. Chappell	Bowled			
			250	O'Keeffe	Ct–f	0		
			251	Walker	Bowled		3–16	
			252	(6) Hookes	Ct–f			1–38
70	1977 v. Aus	Lord's	253	(6) Serjeant	Ct–f			
			254	(4) Walters	Ct–f		0–42	2–16
71		Manchester	255	Walker	Bowled		1–53	
			256	(3) G. Chappell	Bowled			
			257	(4) Serjeant	Ct–f			
			258	Marsh	Ct–f			
			259	Bright	Ct & B	0		
			260	Walker	Ct–f			
			261	Thomson	Ct–f			→ 6–66
72		Nottingham	262	(2) Davis	Ct–f		1–18	
			263	(6) Robinson	LBW			
			264	Pascoe	Ct–f	0		2–49
73		Leeds		Nil				0–16
74		Oval	265	(3) G. Chappell	Ct & B		1–102	
75	1979–80 v. Aus	Perth	266	(5) Hughes	Ct–f		1–33	
			267	(2) Laird	Ct–w/k			
			268	(1) Wiener	Ct–f			
			269	(4) G. Chappell	Stumped			3–82
76		Sydney	270	(4) G. Chappell	Ct–w/k			
			271	Higgs	Bowled		2–39	
			272	(1) Wiener	Bowled			
			273	(3) I. Chappell	Ct–f			
			274	(2) McCosker	Ct–w/k			3–71
77		Melbourne	275	(1) McCosker	Ct–f			
			276	(2) Laird	Ct–f			
			277	(3) I. Chappell	Ct & B		3–131	
			278	(2) Laird	Ct–f			1–49

Test no.	Series	Centre	Victim no.	Batsmen out & how	1st Inns	2nd Inns
78	1980 v. Ind	Bombay		Nil	0–23	
				Nil		0–5

Breakdown of Batsmen Dismissed

105 wickets in 29 Tests of 31 Australians	(Average: 3·62 wkts/Test)
52 ,, ,, 14 ,, ,, 20 Indians	(Average: 3·71 wkts/Test)
48 ,, ,, 8 ,, ,, 17 New Zealanders	(Average: 6·00 wkts/Test)
37 ,, ,, 16 ,, ,, 23 West Indians	(Average: 2·31 wkts/Test)
36 ,, ,, 11 ,, ,, 14 Pakistanis	(Average: 3·27 wkts/Test)
TOTAL: 278 wickets in 78 Tests of 105 players	(Average: 3·58 wkts/Test)

Frequency of Dismissals

13 times: Greg Chappell (Australia)
12 times: Doug Walters (Australia)
10 times: Sunil Gavaskar (India), Ian Chappell (Australia)
9 times: Rod Marsh (Australia)
8 times: Ian Redpath (Australia)
7 times: Mushtaq Mohammad (Pakistan)
6 times: Gundappa Viswanath (India)
5 times: Farokh Engineer (India), Intikhab Alam (Pakistan), Bevan Congdon, Victor Pollard, Glenn Turner and Ken Wadsworth (all 4 New Zealand)
4 times: Johnnie Gleeson, Paul Sheahan and Keith Stackpole (all 3 Australia), Clive Lloyd (West Indies), Dick Motz (New Zealand), Brijesh Patel and Prasanna (both India), Majid Khan (Pakistan)
3 times: Ross Edwards, Bob Inverarity, Jeff Thomson, Max Walker, Bruce Laird and Rick McCosker (all 6 Australia), Alvin Kallicharran and Deryck Murray (both West Indies), Bob Cunis, Graham Dowling, Hedley Howarth, Mike Shrimpton and Bruce Taylor (all 5 New Zealand), Syed Kirmani and Eknath Solkar (both India), Asif Iqbal, Wasim Bari and Zaheer Abbas (all 3 Pakistan)
2 times: Alan Connolly, Terry Jenner, Graham McKenzie, J. Wiener, Ashley Mallett and Craig Serjeant (all 6 Australia), Roy Fredericks, Larry Gomes, Gordon Greenidge, Vanburn Holder, Michael Holding, Rohan Kanhai and Gary Sobers (all 7 West Indies), Dayle Hadlee and Russ Morgan (both New Zealand), Mohinder Amarnath, Dilip Sardesai, Parthasarathy Sharma and Venkataraghavan (all 4 India), Hanif Mohammad, Saeed Ahmed and Wasim Raja (all 3 Pakistan)
1 time: Ray Bright, Ian Davis, Eric Freeman, Gary Gilmour, Jim Higgs, David Hookes, Kim Hughes, Dennis Lillee, Kerry O'Keeffe, Len Pascoe and Richard Robinson (all 11 Australia), Keith Boyce, Basil Butcher, Steve Camacho, Wayne Daniel, Charlie Davis, Maurice Foster, Inshan Ali, Bernard Julien, Collis King, Vivian Richards, Andy Roberts, Lawrence Rowe and John Shepherd (all 13 West Indies), Mark Burgess, Brian Hastings, Geoff Howarth, Bruce Murray and John Parker (all 5 New Zealand), Surinder Amarnath, Bishan Bedi, Chetan Chauhan, Anshuman Gaekwad, Kersan Ghavri, Ashok Mankad, Mansur Ali Khan Pataudi, Ajit Wadekar and Yajurvindrasinh (all 9 India), Aftab Gul, Imran Khan, Javed Burki, Salahuddin and Sarfraz Nawaz (all 5 Pakistan).

Underwood's Modes of Dismissal

Australians Only				*Percentage of Total Dismissals*
48	ct–f	128	Caught by fielder	46%
28	bowled	75	Bowled	27%
9	LBW	24	LBW	9%
11	ct–w/k	25	Caught by Wicketkeeper	9%
7	ct & b	19	Caught and Bowled	7%
2	stp	7	Stumped	2%
105	TOTAL:	278		100%

Analysis of Dismissals

Australians Only			*Percentage*
67	173	Snick or mis-hit (Caught by fielder, wicketkeeper or own bowling)	62%
38	105	Missed the ball (Bowled or LBW or Stumped)	38%
105	TOTAL: 278		100%

Underwood's Victims in the Top Six of Batting Order

Underwood's Test bag is stuffed with some of the finest batsmen in the opposing teams – very nearly two-thirds of them in the top six batting positions. His most notable performance qualitatively was on the 1974–5 tour of Australia. His tally of 16 victims in the top six of the batting order out of a total of 17 dismissals in that rubber is a staggering achievement. Only one genuine lower-order batsman has been pushed up among the top six as a 'night-watchman' – Prasanna at Madras in 1976–7. This solitary instance has been weeded out from the Table hereunder so as to give a precise picture of the extremely high quality of Underwood's bowling:

	Total Number of Wickets	Wickets of the Top Six	Average Percentage of Top Six Dismissals
Australia	105	71	67·61%
West Indies	37	21	56·75%
New Zealand	48	27	56·25%
India	52	37	71·15%
Pakistan	36	22	61·11%
TOTAL	278	178	64·02%

NB: If Prasanna is included, India's total will be 38 for a proportional average of 73·07%. The total will then be 167 with an average of 63·01%.

Underwood's Ducklings: Batsmen Dismissed Without Scoring

	Total Dismissals for a Duck	Ducks among the Top Six	Average Percentage Top Six Duck Dismissals
Australia	10	2	20·00%
West Indies	4	1	25·00%
New Zealand	11	5	45·45%
India	2	1	50·00%
Pakistan	6	3	50·00%
TOTAL	33	12	36·36%

The Top Six Ducklings:

Australia – Ian Chappell, Paul Sheahan.
West Indies – Clive Lloyd
New Zealand – Bevan Congdon, Brian Hastings, Russ Morgan, Vic Pollard, Mike Shrimpton
India – Prasanna ('night-watchman' at no. 5 in second innings at Madras 1976–7)
Pakistan – Asif Iqbal, Mushtaq Mohammad (twice).

Underwood's Happy Hunting Grounds: Breakdown of Test Centres

Total Tests	Tests Played	Centre	Wickets Taken	Total Wickets
	10	The Oval	45	
	8	Lord's	37	
	9	Leeds	24	
	4	Manchester	14	
	5	Nottingham	14	
	5	Birmingham	10	
	—		—	
41		In England		144
	3	Bombay	12	
	2	Delhi	9	
	2	Calcutta	7	
	1	Madras	6	
	1	Bangalore	5	
	1	Kanpur	5	
10	—	In India	—	44
	1	Perth	4	
	2	Adelaide	13	
	4	Sydney	15	
	2	Brisbane	8	
	5	Melbourne	10	
14	—	In Australia	—	50
	2	Christchurch	14	
	2	Auckland	10	
4	—	In New Zealand	—	24
	1	Dacca	6	
	2	Lahore	5	
	1	Hyderabad	0	
	1	Karachi	–	
5	—	In Pakistan	—	11
	2	Port of Spain	4	
	1	Georgetown	1	
	1	Kingston	0	
4	—	In West Indies	—	5
78		GRAND TOTAL		278

Appendix 2. England's Three- and Four-Day Matches during the Australia Tour 1979–80

ENGLAND v. SOUTH AUSTRALIA

Played at Adelaide, 4–6 December 1979. **Match drawn.**

ENGLAND XI

G. Boycott	c and b Sleep	110	(8) not out	63
*J. M. Brearley	c Nash b Sleep	81		
P. Willey	not out	32	(1) c Robertson b Prior	13
G. Miller	not out	26	(7) c Darling b Sleep	71
W. Larkins	did not bat		(2) c sub b Mallett	19
D. I. Gower	did not bat		(3) lbw b Sleep	27
D. L. Bairstow	did not bat		(4) lbw b Prior	12
†R. W. Taylor	did not bat		(5) c Nash b Mallett	0
I. T. Botham	did not bat		(6) lbw b Prior	4
G. B. Stevenson	did not bat		(9) not out	15
Extras	(LB2, NB1)	3	(B3)	3
Total	(2 wkts dec.)	252	(7 wkts dec.)	227

Fall of wickets: 1–174, 2–199. — 1–16, 2–54, 3–64, 4–72, 5–76, 6–76, 7–207.

SOUTH AUSTRALIA

W. M. Darling	lbw b Miller	45	not out	75
J. E. Nash	hit wkt b Botham	48	c Taylor b Lever	0
*I. M. Chappell	c Bairstow b Botham	0	b Stevenson	19
J. I. Crowe	not out	78	b Willey	55
P. R. Sleep	c Boycott b Stevenson	29	not out	30
J. R. Hammond	not out	17		
†P. J. Robertson	did not bat			
G. R. Attenborough	did not bat			
A. A. Mallett	did not bat			
W. Prior	did not bat			
R. M. McLellan	did not bat			
Extras	(LB9)	9	(LB1, NB1)	2
Total	(4 wkts dec.)	226	(3 wkts)	181

Fall of wickets: 1–93, 2–93, 3–93, 4–153. — 1–1, 2–41, 3–112.

BOWLING

SOUTH AUSTRALIA	O	M	R	W	O	M	R	W
Prior	11	2	34	0	13	3	27	3
McLellan	17	2	61	0	9	4	24	0
Hammond	11	2	15	0	10	2	27	0
A. Henborough	6	0	30	0	12	2	39	0
Sleep	26	7	82	2	22.5	8	62	2
Chappell	1	1	0	0				
Mallett	12	3	27	0	22	7	45	2
ENGLAND								
Lever	22	7	44	0	11	0	53	1
Botham	16	4	43	2	4	1	12	0
Stevenson	13	2	41	1	10	2	31	1
Miller	21	7	42	1	6	1	19	0
Willey	11	4	36	0	16	0	60	1
Larkins	4	0	11	0	2	0	4	0

ENGLAND v. QUEENSLAND

Played at Brisbane, 28–31 December. **England won by 138 runs.**

ENGLAND

D. W. Randall	c Langley b Rackemann	0	c Phillips b Balcam	42
W. Larkins	c Langley b Schuller	5	c Phillips b Balcam	19
G. A. Gooch	c sub b Rackemann	115	c Morgan b Cosier	53
P. Willey	c Phillips b Rackemann	30	not out	101
*I. T. Botham	c Parker b Hohns	21	c Langley b Hohns	5
D. I. Gower	c Phillips b Schuller	3	b Hohns	13
†R. W. Taylor	c Hohns b Cosier	32	b Cosier	3
J. E. Emburey	b Schuller	50	c Langley b Hohns	5
G. L. Stevenson	c Langley b Balcam	33	b Cosier	0
G. R. Dilley	c Phillips b Balcam	17		
J. K. Lever	not out	4	(10) not out	16
Extras	(B4, LB4, W1, NB5)	14	(B6, LB3, W2, NB6)	17
Total		324	(8 wkts dec.)	274

Fall of wickets: 1–0, 2–6, 3–83, 4–120, 5–148, 6–194, 7–253, 8–283, 9–311, 10–324.

1–54, 2–77, 3–161, 4–178, 5–214, 6–225, 7–236, 8–237.

QUEENSLAND

*G. J. Cosier	run out	13	c Randall b Stevenson	3
W. G. Morgan	c Taylor b Lever	50	c Gooch b Lever	28
A. D. Ogilvie	b Gooch	5	b Emburey	42
T. V. Hohns	b Emburey	1	(6) c Emburey b Willey	10
J. N. Langley	c Taylor b Lever	5	(4) c Larkins b Willey	16
W. R. Broad	c Randall b Emburey	53	(5) c Botham b Emburey	45
A. D. Parker	not out	52	b Willey	9
†R. B. Phillips	c Taylor b Stevenson	12	c Gower b Emburey	29
D. C. Schuller	c Botham b Emburey	36	c Gower b Lever	25
L. F. Balcam	b Willey	1	absent injured	
C. G. Rackemann	c Taylor b Willey	5	(10) not out	4
Extras	(NB4)	4	(B10, LB2)	12
Total		237		223

Fall of wickets: 1–19, 2–30, 3–35, 4–67, 5–89, 6–138, 7–163, 8–212, 9–221, 10–237.

1–4, 2–41, 3–83, 4–113, 5–140, 6–154, 7–162, 8–201, 9–223.

BOWLING

QUEENSLAND	*O*	*M*	*R*	*W*	*O*	*M*	*R*	*W*
Rackemann	22	5	72	3	9	1	35	0
Schuller	27	3	73	3	7	0	31	1
Balcam	9.4	1	41	2	8	1	54	1
Cosier	8	3	14	1	19	1	43	3
Hohns	32	8	87	1	26.3	3	94	3
Broad	5	1	23	0	1	1	0	0
ENGLAND								
Lever	15	3	39	2	12	5	25	2
Stevenson	14	4	43	1	4	0	29	1
Gooch	4	2	6	1				
Emburey	28	7	80	3	39.2	11	89	3
Willey	13	1	65	2	31	9	68	3

ENGLAND v. NEW SOUTH WALES

Played at Canberra, 27–29 January. **England won by 8 wickets.**

NEW SOUTH WALES

J. Dyson	b Stevenson	5	b Stevenson	45
A. M. Hilditch	c Underwood b Stevenson	21	c Taylor b Underwood	78
T. M. Chappell	c Taylor b Stevenson	6	not out	70
I. C. Davis	c Gooch b Stevenson	2	not out	37
P. M. Toohey	c Taylor b Underwood	38		
*K. D. Walters	b Lever	62		
G. A. Beard	c sub b Emburey	27		
†S. J. Rixon	not out	31		
G. F. Lawson	not out	17		
R. P. Done	did not bat			
R. G. Holland	did not bat			
Extras	(B1, LB1, W1)	3	(LB8, NB5)	13
Total	(7 wkts dec.)	212	(2 wkts dec.)	243

Fall of wickets: 1–10, 2–28, 3–36, 4–37, 5–99, 6–154, 7–182. 1–112, 2–162.

ENGLAND

G. A. Gooch	b Beard	28	(3) not out	73
G. Boycott	c Rixon b Lawson	2	(1) c Toohey b Beard	51
W. Larkins	c Hilditch b Lawson	0	(2) c Toohey b Done	90
D. I. Gower	c Rixon b Done	3	(4) not out	35
*J. M. Brearley	c Beard b Done	24		
D. W. Randall	c and b Beard	44		
†R. W. Taylor	not out	47		
J. E. Emburey	c Toohey b Holland	8		
G. B. Stevenson	b Holland	16		
J. K. Lever	b Holland	0		
D. L. Underwood	b Lawson	16		
Extras	(B2, LB4, NB9)	15	(LB4, NB1)	5
Total		203	(2 wkts)	254

Fall of wickets: 1–7, 2–10, 3–26, 4–53, 5–89, 6–126, 7–143, 8–165, 9–165, 10–203. 1–124, 2–169.

BOWLING

ENGLAND	*O*	*M*	*R*	*W*	*O*	*M*	*R*	*W*
Lever	18	4	42	1	21	3	68	0
Stevenson	15	2	44	4	12	1	47	1
Gooch	4	0	15	0	2	0	11	0
Underwood	23	4	49	1	24	5	50	1
Emburey	20	0	59	1	24	7	54	0
NEW SOUTH WALES								
Lawson	15.5	3	55	3	7	1	17	0
Done	13	5	24	2	13	1	67	1
Beard	20	8	40	2	19	2	65	1
Holland	24	8	62	3	17	3	76	0
Chappell	4	2	7	0	2	0	6	0
Walters					3	1	14	0
Toohey					0.2	0	4	0

ENGLAND v. QUEENSLAND

Played at Brisbane, 12–14 November. **Match drawn**

ENGLAND XI

D. W. Randall	c Madders b Rackemann	97	c G. Chappell b Thomson	7
G. Boycott	c G. Chappell b Schuller	11	c Madders b Schuller	20
D. I. Gower	c G. Chappell b Schuller	2	c Thomson b Schuller	50
G. A. Gooch	c Kent b Rackemann	11	c Thomson b Rackemann	9
P. Willey	lbw b Cosier	1	not out	57
*J. M. Brearley	c Cosier b Rackemann	16	c Kent b Rackemann	5
G. R. Miller	c Broad b Rackemann	16	not out	57
†D. L. Bairstow	c Thomson b Carlson	1		
G. R. Dilley	not out	4		
J. K. Lever	c Madders b Rackemann	0		
M. Hendrick	b Broad	1		
Extras	(B1, LB3, W7, NB5)	16	(B6, LB6, W6, NB3)	21
Total		176	(5 wkts dec.)	226

Fall of wickets: 1–46, 2–53, 3–84, 4–96, 5–154, 6–159, 7–170, 8–175, 9–175, 10–176. 1–16, 2–77, 3–99, 4–101, 5–117.

QUEENSLAND

K. C. Wessels	c Gooch b Lever	2		
W. R. Broad	c Willey b Dilley	6	(2) not out	34
M. F. Kent	c and b Miller	58	(1) c Gooch b Dilley	12
*G. S. Chappell	c Bairstow b Dilley	12	(3) not out	49
G. J. Cosier	c Gooch b Lever	43		
P. Harrison	c Gooch b Dilley	2		
T. D. Hohns	run out	62		
†G. J. Madders	c Lever b Willey	19		
D. C. Schuller	not out	2		
C. J. Rackemann	c Brearley b Miller	3		
Extras	(B3, LB1, W1, NB5)	10	(LB2)	2
Total	(9 wkts dec.)	219	(1 wkt)	97

Fall of wickets: 1–3, 2–15, 3–45, 4–102, 5–113, 6–140, 7–208, 8–214, 9–219. 1–14.

BOWLING

QUEENSLAND	*O*	*M*	*R*	*W*	*O*	*M*	*R*	*W*
Thomson	8	1	26	0	18	6	46	1
Rackemann	14	7	25	5	18	8	35	2
Schuller	12	2	39	2	18	4	54	2
Carlson	11.2	1	38	1				
Cosier	10	2	17	1	10	2	20	0
Hohns	4	0	15	0	19	6	46	0
Broad	1.1	1	0	1	1	1	0	0
Chappell					6	3	4	0
ENGLAND XI								
Lever	18	6	43	2	6	1	14	0
Dilley	15	3	40	3	3.1	0	16	1
Hendrick	4	1	14	0				
Gooch	8	3	16	0	4	0	26	0
Miller	21	5	47	2	7	0	22	0
Willey	12	1	30	1	7	0	17	0
Boycott	4	0	19	0				

ENGLAND v. NORTHERN NEW SOUTH WALES

Played at Newcastle, 17 November. **England won by 9 wickets.**

Northern New South Wales 133 (Beatty 67, Dilley 3–22; Underwood 3–30).

England 136–1 (Boycott 78, Larkins 38 n.o,).

Played at Newcastle, 18 November. **England won by 32 runs.**

England 213–7 (Brearley 67, Larkins 51).

Northern New South Wales 181–7 (Underwood 3–17).

ENGLAND v. COMBINED UNIVERSITIES

(This match was not first-class)

Played at Adelaide, 22–25 November. **Match drawn.**

ENGLAND XI

G. Boycott	c Welham b Burnett	12	c Clough b Kirkwood (retired hurt on 3)	41
W. Larkins	b Hearne	26	(6) b Kirkwood	14
D. W. Randall	c Beatty b Kirkwood	61	(7) c Timms b Kirkwood	0
G. A. Gooch	c Burnett b Clough	18	(3) c Timms b Burnett	124
I. T. Botham	c Hearne b Kirkwood	8	c Davies b Clough	76
*J. M. Brearley	c Kirkwood b Clough	1	(2) c Timms b Clough	11
P. Willey	c Welham b Burnett	28	(4) c Welham b Kirkwood	34
†R. W. Taylor	c and b Kirkwood	11	not out	66
J. K. Lever	b Kirkwood	2	b Hearne	37
D. L. Underwood	c Burnett b Kirkwood	4	not out	3
R. G. D. Willis	not out	2		
Extras	(B1, LB1, W2, NB2)	6	(B2, LB2, W1)	5
Total		179	(8 wkts)	411

Fall of wickets: 1–18, 2–47, 3–84, 4–92, 5–94, 6–144, 7–162, 8–164, 9–174, 10–179.

1–16, 2–86, 3–221, 4–261, 5–286, 6–287, 7–306, 8–402.

COMBINED UNIVERSITIES

P. J. Davies	c Boycott b Botham	4	(2) c Gooch b Underwood	20
P. D. Whitehead	c Larkins b Underwood	24	(1) lbw b Willis	57
D. M. Welham	c Botham b Underwood	21	c Botham b Boycott	95
*J. B. Robson	lbw b Underwood	0	c Taylor b Underwood	3
C. Beatty	c and b Underwood	53	b Underwood	35
M. Burgess	c Taylor b Botham	5	not out	8
†P. Timms	c Larkins b Underwood	4		
G. Kirkwood	c Willey b Underwood	37		
J. R. Hearne	not out	12		
I. K. Burnett	b Underwood	0		
P. M. Clough	c Taylor b Underwood	0		
Extras	(LB5, NB3)	8	(LB8, NB1)	9
Total		168	(5 wkts)	227

Fall of wickets: 1–6, 2–49, 3–49, 4–52, 5–59, 6–66, 7–140, 8–167, 9–167, 10–168.

1–53, 2–109, 3–129, 4–200, 5–227.

BOWLING

COMBINED UNIVERSITIES	O	M	R	W	O	M	R	W
Clough	18	4	49	2	26	6	72	2
Burnett	14	3	42	2	23	2	105	1
Hearne	10	2	30	1	25	4	104	1
Kirkwood	16.3	5	52	5	22	3	96	4
Beatty	2	2	0	0	10	1	29	0

ENGLAND	O	M	R	W	O	M	R	W
Willis	14	4	28	0	13	4	29	1
Botham	15	4	39	2	9	2	28	0
Lever	18	6	35	0	14	2	45	0
Underwood	23.5	8	41	8	24	7	50	3
Willey	11	4	17	0	17	5	31	0
Gooch					7	2	20	0
Larkins					4	1	5	0
Boycott					2.3	0	9	1

ENGLAND v. TASMANIA

Played at Hobart, 30 November, 1–2 December. **England won by 100 runs.**

ENGLAND

G. Boycott	not out	101		
W. Larkins	st Woolley b Goodman	21	(3) not out	8
D. W. Randall	c Goodman b Campbell	34		
G. A. Gooch	c Hadlee b Campbell	51	(1) not out	70
D. I. Gower	did not bat		(2) b Campbell	53
G. Miller	did not bat			
†R. W. Taylor	did not bat			
G. R. Dilley	did not bat			
D. L. Underwood	did not bat			
J. K. Lever	did not bat			
*R. G. D. Willis	did not bat			
Extras	(LB4, NB3)	7	(B2, W1, NB1)	4
Total	(3 wkts dec.)	214	(1 wkt dec.)	135

Fall of wickets: 1–37, 2–126, 3–214. 1–102.

TASMANIA

G. Goodman	not out	28	run out	8
R. Knight	c Dilley b Underwood	22	c Lever b Underwood	74
B. Campbell	lbw b Underwood	9	(8) c Gower b Miller	0
D. Smith	c Taylor b Underwood	2	(3) c Larkins b Underwood	0
D. Boon	not out	6	(4) c Gower b Underwood	35
*R. Davison	did not bat		(5) lbw b Underwood	15
†R. Woolley	did not bat		(6) c Miller b Underwood	24
T. Dorking	did not bat		(7) c sub (Stevenson) b Underwood	0
R. Hadlee	did not bat		c Gooch b Underwood	14
G. Wilson	did not bat		b Miller	0
P. Blizzard	did not bat		not out	2
Extras	(B2, NB2)	4	(B3, NB3)	6
Total	(3 wkts dec.)	71		178

Fall of wickets: 1–34, 2–59, 3–64. 1–47, 2–48, 3–91, 4–125, 5–136, 6–138, 7–167, 8–168, 9–178, 10–178.

BOWLING

TASMANIA	*O*	*M*	*R*	*W*	*O*	*M*	*R*	*W*
Hadlee	13	6	17	0	5	1	16	0
Blizzard	17	5	49	0	5	1	21	0
Wilson	11	2	25	0	7	0	31	0
Goodman	23	7	59	1	5	1	37	0
Campbell	16.5	1	57	2	4.5	0	26	1
ENGLAND								
Dilley	10	2	24	0	7	1	20	0
Lever	8	3	17	0	1	0	1	0
Willis	8	2	15	0	7	2	13	0
Underwood	15.1	11	11	3	30.4	12	66	7
Miller					30	5	72	2